HORARY ASTROLOGY

THE PRACTICAL WAY TO LEARN

YOUR FATE

Radical Charts for Student and Professional

Petros Eleftheriadis

The Wessex Astrologer

Published in 2017 by
The Wessex Astrologer Ltd
4A Woodside Road
Bournemouth
BH5 2AZ
www.wessexastrologer.com

Cover Design by Jonathan Taylor

A catalogue record for this book is available at The British Library

ISBN 9781910531211

Contents

Glossary

Accidental dignities/debilities: Planets gain power when they are placed in fortunate houses, when they have a good relationship with the Sun or the other planets and when they are direct and faster than average. They are weak when the opposite is true. For more information, see the Table of Accidental dignities on p.4.

Almuten of a house: The planet that has the most essential dignity in the degree of the cusp of a house.

Antiscium: A planet has its antiscium in the degree that has the same distance as him from the 0° Cancer/0° Capricorn axis on the other side of it. So, 28° Gemini has a two degree distance from 0° Cancer. 2° Cancer also has a two degree distance from 0° Cancer. A planet at 28° Gemini, therefore, has its antiscium at 2° Cancer. If another planet is found at 2° Cancer, then these two planets at 28° Gemini and 2° Cancer are believed to be in some sort of a conjunction.

Benefic: Any planet that has sufficient essential and/or accidental dignity.

Besiegement: A planet is besieged when he is positioned between the two Infortunes and this is negative. For a planet positioned between the two Fortunes, which is positive, I prefer the term enclosure.

Cazimi: A planet is said to be cazimi when he is in the heart of the Sun, only 17' minutes away from him. This is considered to be very fortunate for the planet.

Combust planet: A planet that has an 8°– 8°30' degree distance from the Sun from either side. This is a most serious debility.

Diurnal chart: A chart where the Sun is above the horizon, that is, the 1st/7th house axis.

Essential dignities/debilities: Planets have power or can function better in certain signs or degrees of every sign (dignities). Likewise, planets cannot function properly in certain signs (debilities).

Fortunes: Jupiter and Venus. Jupiter is the Fortune of sect in diurnal charts and Venus is the Fortune of sect in nocturnal charts.

Hayz: A diurnal planet is said to be in hayz when he is diurnally placed (in the same side as the Sun) in a diurnal chart and in a diurnal sign. A nocturnal planet is in hayz when he is nocturnally placed (in the opposite side of the Sun) in a nocturnal chart and in a nocturnal sign.

Infortunes: Saturn and Mars. Saturn is the Infortune of sect in diurnal charts and Mars is the Infortune of sect in nocturnal charts.

Intercepted sign: A sign that is wholly included in a house.

Joy of the planets (houses): Mercury rejoices in the 1st house, the Moon in the 3rd house, Venus in the 5th house, Mars in the 6th house, the Sun in the 9th house, Jupiter in the 11th house and Saturn in the 12th house.

Malefic: Saturn or Mars without dignity nor strongly received.

Moiety: Planets have orbs. For an aspect to be particularly effective, it has to be within the moiety (half) of the two planets' orbs. For example, Saturn has a 10 degree orb and Jupiter a 12 degree orb. For an aspect between these two to be effective, it has to be within (10+12/2 = 11) an 11 degree orb.

Moon void in/of course: The Moon is void in/of course when she makes no applying aspect before she leaves the sign she is in.

Nocturnal chart: A chart where the Sun is below the horizon, that is, the 1st/7th house axis.

Occidental planet: A planet that sets after the Sun.

Oriental planet: A planet that rises before the Sun.

Partill aspect: An aspect is partill when the two planets in aspect are in the same degree in their respective signs. For example, the Moon in 23° Pisces makes a partill trine with Jupiter at 23° Cancer.

Peregrine: A planet that is in none of his own dignities. This is considered to be a debility. However, if the planet is received, this is not a problem.

Querent: The person who asks the question.

Quesited: The thing/person asked about.

Reception: When a planet is in the dignities of another planet, we say that the other planet receives him. In a single reception, an aspect is required for the other planet to offer his help to the received one. In a mutual reception, apparently no aspect is needed, although, naturally, it works a lot better with an aspect. In this case (no aspect), the term mutual generosity is often preferred, instead of mutual reception.

Under the beams: A planet is under the beams when he is 17 degrees away from the Sun, either applying or separating. It's a debility, but not as serious as combustion.

Via Combusta: The area of the zodiac between 15 degrees of Libra and 15 degrees of Scorpio. This may be a negative testimony when the Moon is found there, but I do not believe that the chart is unreadable when that happens.

Table of Accidental Dignities and Debilities

Accidental Fortitudes		Accidental Debilities	
In the midheaven or ascendant	5	In the 12th house	- 5
In the 7th,4th or 11th houses	4	In the 8th and 6th	- 2
In the 2nd and 5th	3		
In the 9th	2		
In the 3rd house	1		
Direct (the ☉ and ☽ are always direct)	4	Retrograde	- 5
Swift in motion	2	Slow in motion	- 2
♄ ♃ ♂ when oriental	2	♄ ♃ ♂ occidental	- 2
☿ and ♀ when occidental	2	☿ and ♀ oriental	- 2
☽ increasing, or when occidental	2	☽ decreasing in light	- 2
Free from combustion and ☉ beams	5	Combust of the ☉	- 5
In the heart of the ☉, or cazimi	5	Under the ☉ beams	- 4
In partill conj. with ♃ and ♀	5	Partill conj. with ♄ or ♂	- 5
In partill conj. with ☊	4	Partill conj. with ☋	- 4
In partill trine to ♃ and ♀	4	Besieged between ♄ and ♂	- 5
In partill sextile to ♃ and ♀	3	Partill opp. with ♄ or ♂	- 4
In conj. with Cor Leonis	6	Partill square with ♄ or ♂	- 3
Or in conj. with Spica	5	In conj. with Caput Algol	- 5

Introduction

I believe in fate. I'm being straightforward here. I didn't use to, but the more I got involved with astrology and horary astrology in particular, it became evident that no other explanation was possible IF astrology works. And it does work. Which means that if you can cast a chart that will give an accurate answer as to whether your lost pet is OK and the chart tells you that it is and it's going to come back home in three days, then everything is written in the stars, I'm afraid. I know you don't like it, but there you have it.

This realization however has changed my practice. I don't accept questions that are attempting to change a client's fate, nor do I believe that they are valid. "Should I take job A or job B? Which is better?" It doesn't matter, your natal chart may indicate that you are going through a tough professional period and this means that you HAVE TO take the "bad" job. There is no choice here. *Astrology charts cannot possibly show something that will NEVER materialize, something that will never become reality, so they cannot show how your life would be, had you made another decision.* What's more, astrology cannot make your decisions for you. It may be that those decisions have already been made before your body was born, but this doesn't alter the fact that YOU have to execute them.

Imagine going to an astrologer every time when something important is at stake. What are you really asking the astrologer to do for you? You are asking the astrologer to save you from the pain of being incarnated. Let's say that the astrologer tells you, for example, that you shouldn't form a relationship with a certain person, because it will end in tears. But, this is exactly what's supposed to happen. You should have the experience of a relationship that will hurt you badly and will scar you forever. This is what your natal chart indicates. Who told you that we are here to be happy? We are here to experience life, nothing more than that, and the kind of life that we are going to have is indicated by our natal chart. Lilly always said the natal chart comes first, so perhaps we should follow his advice.

Unfortunately, most people go to an astrologer nowadays, either because they want to change something or avoid something. For example, a client hasn't written a book, but he asks the astrologer if it's going to be published, so as not to write it if the answer is negative. Invalid question. Other examples: "If I apply for this job, will I get it?" Invalid question. First apply for the job and then ask the question. "Will I win, if I play the lottery?" If your natal chart doesn't show such a win, no matter how many charts you cast and no matter how wonderful they are, you are not going to win. It's as simple as that and all those wonderful charts are simply invalid.

There are people who believe in fate, but accept this kind of question because they say that going to an astrologer is part of the client's fate, so it's OK to answer "Should I?" questions. Perhaps, but what about the astrologer's fate? Is spreading the lie that there is free will part of his or her fate? If one believes in free will, fine (although how one who has this belief can make predictions is beyond me), but if one doesn't, are they sure their natal chart indicates that they should go on lying to people? Natal charts are not as clear as horary charts and it's often difficult to make judgements on such subtle issues. So, one needs to make a "choice", even if that choice has already been made before one was born. I, therefore, made a choice to not answer such questions.

So, what's the purpose of going to an astrologer, I hear you ask? If you want to know your future in order to change it, then simply don't go to an astrologer, it's pointless. Astrology, however, is extremely important in helping you embrace your fate, in helping you realize, time and time again, that you are part of a great design. Have you seen the film *Stranger than Fiction*? Despite its Hollywood ending, which is understandable, I think it explains very well what fate is and how astrology works, without ever mentioning astrology. When the hero finds out exactly his life story, he realizes how perfect it all is, in spite of its sad and unfortunate parts, and he doesn't want to change a thing. This is exactly what astrology can do for us, it helps us realize the old cliché "everything happens for a reason".

Consequently, in this book, I do not include "Should I?" charts, nor do I include any charts that are not radical, following the major considerations before judgement (I make only a few exceptions, but I explain why). Lilly seems sometimes to ignore these considerations, but it was difficult to send a client away in those days. Nowadays, when it is so easy to cast a chart and communicate with a client, we have no excuse. A lot of charts are invalid, either because there is no real question behind them or because the client doesn't ask what he/she really wants to know. People sometimes say that considerations before judgement make no sense, because it's like saying that astrology sometimes works and sometimes it doesn't. No, it's not that at all. Remember, we are talking about horary astrology here, not natal. When a child is born, their chart is valid, because a birth actually took place, the child is real. The child, however, becomes real at the moment of birth, not at conception. Just because someone has conceived a child, this doesn't mean that a child will actually be born, as we well know. Horary astrology is like that, but instead of a child, we have the querent's question. With horary astrology we cannot be sure whether the question is real or not, because very often querents can't be trusted. This means that the considerations before judgement are very useful, particularly when more than one is present, in which case, I strongly urge you to cast the chart aside.

The charts included in this book do not cover all possible areas. For example, I've never had an "Am I pregnant?" question in my practice, possibly because people, quite understandably, prefer to take the test or go to the doctor instead of going to an astrologer. However, this is not important. I don't believe in aphorisms and in special rules for each topic. In every chart, no matter what the question is, you do basically the same work: dignities, receptions, aspects.

All the questions about sports are mine (no examples in my professional practice) and there are a few others that are mine as well (questions about elections, song contests, etc.).

One final note: The main objective in horary is to answer questions with a simple YES or NO. The answer may be a single word, but it's not always easy getting there. True, there is a detailed script for all our actions, but it's very difficult for an astrologer to accurately make it out, so simply don't do it, because half of the time you are going to be wrong.

Part 1
Theoretical Approach

This is mainly a book of horary charts for practice, so no theory is going to be presented, as it is taken for granted that you are familiar with the traditional theory. If you are not, I refer you to Barbara Dunn's brilliant and detailed book *Horary Astrology Re–Examined*. However, I feel that certain things need to be said in order for you to understand how I approach the charts providing some information about basic astrological concepts.

Signs

The twelve signs are divided into three categories: moveable (cardinal), fixed and common (double–bodied, mutable). Aries, Cancer, Libra and Capricorn are moveable, Taurus, Leo, Scorpio and Aquarius are fixed and Gemini, Virgo, Sagittarius and Pisces are common. If the significators of a question are in cardinal signs, things happen more quickly, in fixed signs more slowly and in common signs somewhere in the middle. In questions of illness, the significators in fixed signs may show an illness that lasts for a long time, in moveable signs acute diseases that go away quickly and in common signs illnesses that "come and go". Significators in fixed signs often indicate someone who tells the truth and in job questions, people likely to keep their jobs (if other testimonies concur). Common signs, also called double–bodied, indicate that there may be more than one of the quesited (e.g. children) and they often indicate change.

There are four triplicities: The fire triplicity (Aries, Leo, Sagittarius), the air triplicity (Gemini, Libra, Aquarius), the earth triplicity (Taurus, Virgo, Capricorn) and the water triplicity (Cancer, Scorpio, Pisces). In questions of illness, the third sign of the triplicity is the "worst", in the sense that it signifies a very serious condition if the significators are in those signs. The water signs are the most fruitful ones and the significators in those signs in questions of pregnancy or money are a good testimony. Gemini, Leo and Virgo are barren signs, although Gemini and Virgo, if the chart is fortunate in general, can often be an indication of twins. The air signs and Virgo are considered the "humane" signs, the more civilized ones. The air signs are hot and moist by nature, the fire signs hot and dry, the water signs cold and moist and the earth signs cold and dry.

Aries, Gemini, Leo, Libra, Sagittarius and Aquarius are diurnal/masculine signs, while Taurus, Cancer, Virgo, Scorpio, Capricorn and Pisces are nocturnal/feminine signs. This can be useful in questions where the astrologer tries to determine the sex of the baby, for example.

Planets

Jupiter and Venus are the two Fortunes. It's doubtful whether they can become truly malefic. At the very least, a nasty Jupiter is preferable to a nasty Saturn. Jupiter is the greater Fortune and Venus is the lesser Fortune, although sect needs to be taken into account. In diurnal charts, Jupiter is the Fortune of sect and in nocturnal charts, Venus. The two Infortunes are Saturn and Mars. Saturn is the greater Infortune and Mars is the lesser Infortune, although, again, Saturn behaves better in diurnal charts and Mars in nocturnal charts. Out of sect Infortunes can be dangerous if they are also essentially and accidentally debilitated. *It must be stressed that even when the Infortunes are significators, this does not mean that they cease to be Infortunes. In fact, this is by itself a negative testimony.*

In horary charts, besides the principal significators, we often check the natural significators of the quesited who provides supporting testimony. If the question is about money or pregnancy, the astrologer should check Jupiter as well (possibly also Venus for pregnancy, being the natural ruler of the 5th house where she also rejoices). The Moon is the natural significator of property and of the mother in nocturnal charts; Venus rules relationships and marriage and is the natural significator of mothers in diurnal charts; the Sun is the natural significator of many tenth house matters (job, preferment), the natural significator of the father in diurnal charts and the natural significator of men in general in relationship charts; Saturn signifies old people and the father in nocturnal charts; and finally, Mars rules surgery and surgeons in questions of illness and is the natural significator of brothers.

The Sun, Jupiter and Saturn are diurnal planets and they behave better in diurnal charts. The Moon, Venus and Mars are nocturnal planets and so, they prefer nocturnal charts. Mercury is diurnal when oriental of the Sun and nocturnal when occidental of the Sun.

The Role of the Moon

I do not believe that the Moon is only a co–significator of the querent. The Moon is a co–significator of everything in a horary chart, which means that the Moon is also co–significator of the quesited (in the example charts, I mention the Moon as co–significator of the querent when I name the significators, but in the judgement itself it becomes clear that I consider her a co–significator of everything). If the Moon applies to the significator of the querent, this is positive testimony, especially if the aspect is fortunate and there is reception. As for the previous and the next aspect of the Moon being significators of the querent and the quesited, although hardly anyone considers them as such anymore, I believe this concept has some value and it agrees with what I say below about the main significators. I believe that authorities of the past noted that when the Moon's next aspect was positive, the outcome was often successful, so they considered the planet the Moon applies to as significator of the quesited and the planet from whom the Moon separates as significator of the querent (translating in this way the light from querent to quesited). We don't need, however, to call them significators, but I must stress the importance of the good fortune of the whole chart. If the Moon (or the significator of the querent) applies with a fortunate aspect to another planet with reception, this is positive testimony and *it doesn't matter if that other planet is a significator or not*. Likewise, if the aspect is unfortunate and there is no reception, this is negative testimony.

Houses

You can read about the basic meanings of the twelve houses in Barbara's book. I will deal here with some issues regarding houses.

• The house ruler is not only the domicile ruler of the sign on the cusp of the house. Signification is also derived from the almuten or co–almuten (if this is a different planet from the domicile ruler), the planets inside the house and in the same sign as the cusp, the planets in the previous house but conjunct the house cusp, the domicile ruler of the intercepted sign (if there is one) and the planets located in the intercepted sign. Lilly sometimes derived signification from the ruler of the next sign if late degrees of a sign were on a cusp. I'm not sure about this, but I would consider it if the next sign is the correct sign using the whole sign house system. For example, suppose 28° Aries is on the 8th house cusp and 28° Taurus in the 9th house cusp with a Libra ascendant. In this instance, Taurus has more degrees in the 8th house than Aries and Lilly would also consider Venus as a significator for 8th house issues. In this case, so would I, because Taurus is the natural 8th house sign with a Libra ascendant using the whole sign house system. If, however, Taurus didn't have this 8th house relationship with the ascendant, I wouldn't use Venus as a significator.

- There is no relationship between the 8th or the 5th house and sex in traditional astrology. Instead, it is the 7th house that was considered the house of sexual unions (Al Biruni, Masha'allah) and marriage. The 5th house may have some connection with sex (being the house of Venus' joy and which she naturally rules), but I have not found any such reference in the traditional sources. I would suggest that in most cases we don't need a house for sex. Even in questions like "Will we have sex?" joining the 1st and the 7th house significators will suffice.

- I would suggest that there is no need for so much fuss over finding the correct significators. People feel that life has changed a lot since Lilly's day and we do not know which planet or house rules all those things Lilly and the other authors didn't mention, because they did not exist at the time. As it will be shown in the charts below, evaluating the ruler/s of the ascendant and the Moon will most often lead you to the correct answer *no matter what the question is*. If the ruler of the ascendant is debilitated and applying to an Infortune with a hard aspect and the same goes for the Moon, a positive answer is highly unlikely.

- I mainly use the Regiomontanus house system because of Lilly, although I'm more of a fan of Porphyry and Alcabitius and I am considering the transition. I like the idea of the whole sign house system, but I have not found that it works consistently with the MC/IC axis, that may not fall in the 10th/4th house axis accordingly. Still, I could be persuaded otherwise. However, I think it is very important when planets aspect or don't aspect the ascendant. A planet 15 degrees behind the ascendant but in the same sign as the ascendant cannot be called a true 12th house planet. In the chart examples, you may perhaps be surprised when I seem to place planets in different houses than the one they are technically in. *When a planet is in a different sign from the one on the cusp of the house and that sign is not intercepted, I often place the planet in the next house, especially when the aspect agrees.* For example, in a chart with a Scorpio ascendant, the MC in Leo and Mars in Virgo technically in the 10th house, I consider this Mars to have more affinity with the 11th house than the 10th.

Aspects

Trines and sextiles are fortunate and if there is a strong reception they are always effective. Trines can sometimes work without reception (if there is supporting testimony), but sextiles almost always require reception, unless the planets involved are very strong essentially and accidentally. Squares and oppositions are unfortunate. A square ceases to be a problem (or this much of a problem) with a strong mutual reception or if the Fortunes are involved and they are dignified. An opposition never really ceases to be a problem, even when there is a strong mutual reception, although, of course, reception helps.

A conjunction is not an aspect, but it's the strongest possible testimony of perfection. However, it's neither fortunate nor unfortunate and it all depends on whether the planets involved are Fortunes or Infortunes and whether there are receptions or not.

Reception

I use the traditional definition of reception, which means that reception is always positive. Always. There is no such thing as a negative reception. Even in an aspect like Moon in Capricorn opposite Saturn in Cancer, where both planets are in detriment and the aspect is unfortunate, the reception is a good thing; in fact, the only good thing in this configuration. It may not amount to much – that is, it may not provide us with a successful outcome – but it is a positive indication nonetheless.

A single reception, in order for it to be effective, needs to involve an aspect between the two planets. It makes no sense otherwise. If all our planets were received and therefore helped by all of their dispositors, then all our charts would be perfect, which is obviously not the case. In order for a single reception to strengthen a planet, it requires an applying aspect, or, at the very least, a separating aspect but still within the moiety of the planets' orbs. *However, if there is a reception by domicile or exaltation in the same sign (conjunction), I believe that this is very powerful even if the two planets are very far from one another or separating.* For mutual reception, Lilly didn't require an aspect, although it naturally makes a huge difference if there is one.

A strong mutual reception (between domicile and exaltation) can almost completely take away the malice of the square aspect, particularly if there are no Infortunes involved. If the mutual reception is between the two Infortunes and the aspect is a square (e.g. Mars in Aquarius square Saturn in Scorpio), this is undoubtedly good testimony (the absence of reception in this case would have made this aspect extremely negative), but not all problems are erased. A sextile between Mars in Capricorn and Saturn in Scorpio is much better.

A planet cannot receive planets found in his detriment or fall. This is NOT reception. A planet cannot receive another if he has no claim on the sign or degree the other planet is located in. Remember, reception is always a good thing.

The ancient texts (e.g. Al Kindi and others) do mention that a planet applying to another from a sign that is the other planet's detriment or fall (e.g. the Moon in Aries applying to Saturn) is not a positive indication. Or when the planet applied to is in a sign of the applying planet's detriment or fall (e.g. the Moon applying to Saturn in Scorpio). They stress, however, that this is NOT reception. There may be some truth in this, but the astrologer MUST observe if there is also (true) reception in such cases. For example, the Moon in Capricorn applying to Saturn in Scorpio is positive testimony because we have a fortunate aspect with a strong reception and the fact that Saturn in Scorpio doesn't "like" the

Moon is not of major importance. Instead, Saturn receives the Moon in his domicile and will therefore assist her, regardless of whether he actually "likes" her or not.

Translation, Collection, Prohibition, Frustration etc.

A true translation of light occurs when the two planets in question DON'T aspect each other or are separating from an aspect and the third planet intervenes and brings them together. If the two planets are applying to each other, they do not need the third planet's intervention, which could prove to be problematic instead of helpful. If the third planet hasn't yet perfected the aspect with the first planet, then this is also NOT a translation of light between the two planets in question. This doesn't mean that we won't have a fortunate outcome, it simply means that this is not a translation of light.

The same goes for the collection of light. The two planets in question must not aspect each other or they should be separating from one another, but they must both be applying to the heavier planet.

A translation or a collection of light isn't always effective. If the intermediary planet forms hard aspects with the other two planets without reception, or if he is accidentally debilitated (e.g. retrograde, combust), it is doubtful that he can perform the task adequately.

Whenever a third planet intervenes, whether that is technically called prohibition or frustration or whatever, we must always check if this intervention is capable of destroying the matter. Just because a third planet steps in, this doesn't mean that we have a problem. A trine, for example, between the Moon and Jupiter with reception cannot possibly prohibit the matter. A square with Saturn, however, without reception, will almost always prohibit the matter.

Essential dignities, fixed stars, antiscia, void of/in course Moon, considerations before judgement, combustion, cazimi, Moon's Nodes

I use the Dorothean triplicity rulers (Mars as ruler of the water triplicity for both day and night makes no sense to me) and I use the Egyptian terms. (See table on following page.) It is my belief that Ptolemy couldn't understand the logic behind the Egyptian terms and created his own, despite what he says about finding an old manuscript etc. I think

Sign	Houses of the Planets		Exalt-ation	Triplicity of Planets D	N	The Terms of the Planets					The Faces of the Planets			Detriment	Fall
♈	♂	D	☉ 19	☉	♃	♃ 6	♀ 6 (12)	☿ 8 (20)	♂ 5 (25)	♄ 5 (30)	♂ 10	☉ 20	♀ 30	♀	♄
♉	♀	N	☽ 3	♀	☽	♀ 8	☿ 6 (14)	♃ 8 (22)	♄ 5 (27)	♂ 3 (30)	☿ 10	☽ 20	♄ 30	♂	
♊	☿	D	☊ 3	♄	☿	☿ 6	♃ 6 (12)	♀ 5 (17)	♂ 7 (24)	♄ 6 (30)	♃ 10	♂ 20	☉ 30	♃	
♋	☽	D/N	♃ 15	♀	♂	♂ 7	♀ 6 (13)	☿ 6 (19)	♃ 7 (26)	♄ 4 (30)	♀ 10	☿ 20	☽ 30	♄	♂
♌	☉	D/N		☉	♃	♃ 6	♀ 5 (11)	♄ 7 (18)	☿ 6 (24)	♂ 6 (30)	♄ 10	♃ 20	♂ 30	♄	
♍	☿	N	☿ 15	♀	☽	☿ 7	♀ 10 (17)	♃ 4 (21)	♂ 7 (28)	♄ 2 (30)	☉ 10	♀ 20	☿ 30	♃	♀
♎	♀	D	♄ 21	♄	☿	♄ 6	☿ 8 (14)	♃ 7 (21)	♀ 7 (28)	♂ 2 (30)	☽ 10	♄ 20	♃ 30	♂	☉
♏	♂	N		♀	♂	♂ 7	♀ 4 (11)	☿ 8 (19)	♃ 5 (24)	♄ 6 (30)	♂ 10	☉ 20	♀ 30	♀	☽
♐	♃	D	☋ 3	☉	♃	♃ 12	♀ 5 (17)	☿ 4 (21)	♄ 5 (26)	♂ 4 (30)	☿ 10	☽ 20	♄ 30	☿	
♑	♄	N	♂ 28	♀	☽	☿ 7	♃ 7 (14)	♀ 8 (22)	♄ 4 (26)	♂ 4 (30)	♃ 10	♂ 20	☉ 30	☽	♃
♒	♄	D		♄	☿	☿ 7	♀ 6 (13)	♃ 7 (20)	♂ 5 (25)	♄ 5 (30)	♀ 10	☿ 20	☽ 30	☉	
♓	♃	N	♀ 27	♀	♂	♀ 12	♃ 4 (16)	☿ 3 (19)	♂ 9 (28)	♄ 2 (30)	♄ 10	♃ 20	♂ 30	☿	☿

Table of essential dignities using the Dorothean triplicity rulers and the Egyptian terms the Egyptian terms work better and at the end of the book you can find an article I wrote on the subject. I'm also of the opinion that terms is a stronger dignity than triplicity, but this needs further inspection, so in this book I've kept the standard point system (5 for domicile, 4 for exaltation, 3 for triplicity, 2 for terms and 1 for face).

When a planet has some dignity (triplicity and terms, not face) and is also in its detriment or fall, the debility is not so important and dignity takes precedence, especially for the Fortunes. It's still a problem, but not such a big one. A planet in detriment or fall (more in detriment than in fall) is like a civilized person in the jungle. The planet/person without dignity will soon die. The planet/person with dignity is going to find by chance the safest place in the jungle, away from the wild beasts. He is still going to be in the jungle, but in the best possible place there. Dignity provides protection to the planet in detriment or fall.

I have not found the fixed stars particularly useful in the delineation of horary charts. At best, they offer supporting testimony and I would stick to the three stars Lilly mentions (Spica, Regulus, Algol). Regulus, in particular, in questions of success or sport or questions of a similar type, if found on the ascendant or the MC, seems to be a very powerful testimony of success.

I have not found antiscia particularly useful either. If you make the mistake to exclude almutens, if you consider the Moon to be only a co–significator of the querent and if you don't allow planets in houses to be co–significators of the houses they are located, then, yes, you need something extra and you may rely too much on antiscia. In my practice, however, antiscia have rarely played an important part.

I do not usually judge charts that have a void in course Moon, even if it is found in Taurus, Cancer, Sagittarius or Pisces. However, not all void in course Moons are the same. If the Moon is at 28 degrees of a sign, separating from a planet at 27 degrees and applying to a planet at 0 degrees, it is doubtful whether you can actually call this Moon void. In addition, a Moon at 29 degrees is at the end of its void course and if her next aspect is within the moiety of the two planets' orbs, I would judge the chart.

I also do not judge charts that are not radical. I pay particular attention to a combust ascendant ruler (which very often indicates the querent is confused or there is no real question, unless it's a medical chart), early or late degrees ascending (unless perhaps the querent shares the same ascending sign particularly in the same degree as the horary chart) and the void in course Moon. If one of these factors is present, I put the chart aside (for the void in course Moon, see above). With the other considerations I'm more flexible, if there is only one present in the chart. In cases where there are 2–3 considerations present, then I feel that there is no question at all, or at least not the question the querent has in mind.

Combustion is undoubtedly very serious, but I agree with Masha'allah that a strong reception saves from total destruction. When combustion happens in Leo or Aries, the Sun receives the planet he is conjunct with in his domicile or exaltation and does not destroy him. I believe this is better than the other way round, that is, if the planet receives the Sun, for example Sun/Mercury in Virgo, although, of course, Mercury in this case has the strength to fight off some of the Sun's destructive effects. As for cazimi, I cannot say for certain whether it needs to be both by latitude and longitude. I have two examples, one is cazimi by longitude and the other cazimi both by longitude and latitude. They both seemed to work, although other testimonies were also present.

Finally, there have been various suggestions as to how to treat the Nodes of the Moon: a) they are both negative, b) the North Node increases and the South Node decreases the good or evil of every planet and c) the North Node is positive and the South Node is negative. It is this last suggestion (North Node always positive and South Node always negative) that I use in this book.

Part Two
Practical Application

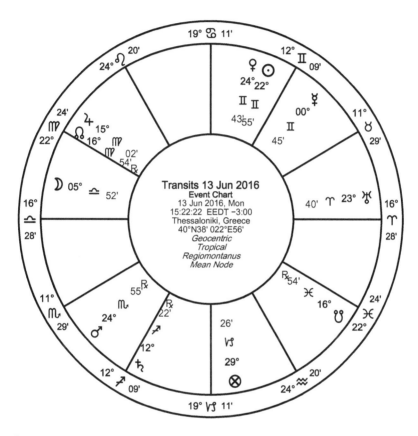

19° ♋ 11'

24° ♌ 20'

12° ♊ 09'

♀ ☉
24° 22'
♊ ♊
43 55'

☿
00°

♊
45'

♃
15°
♏ 16° ♍
02'
54'R

24'
♍
22°

11°
♉
29'

☽ 05° ♎ 52'

16°
♎
28'

Transits 13 Jun 2016
Event Chart
13 Jun 2016, Mon
15:22:22 EEDT −3:00
Thessaloniki, Greece
40°N38' 022°E56'
Geocentric
Tropical
Regiomontanus
Mean Node

40' ♈ 23° ♅

16°
♈
28'

♓ 54'R

16° ♓

55'R
♏
22'R

11°
♏
29'

24°
♂

12°
♐

26'
♑
29°

⊗

♓
24'

☋
22°

24° ♒ 20'

12°
♐
09'
♄

19° ♑ 11'

House systems

At the QHP we use the Regiomontanus house system (although, as I've already said, I have recently taken a liking to Porphyry and Alcabitius). However, you should always have a whole sign approach to house placement, that is, check what relationship the sign each planet is in has with the ascending sign. A planet may very well be in Capricorn in the 5th house, but the good fortune of the 5th house will be greatly reduced if the ascending sign is Leo, therefore not in aspect with the planet in Capricorn.

In the chart shown, there is no problem with Mars, Saturn, Uranus (although at the QHP we don't use outer planets), Venus and the Sun, as there is no doubt as to which house they are located in. What about the rest of the planets? Pluto is obviously a 4th house planet, even if he is located in the 3rd house, because of his close conjunction with the IC and following Ptolemy's five degree rule (we should also be flexible with this). Neptune has a 6th house relationship with the ascendant. Even if you don't want to put him in the 6th house, you cannot escape the fact that he doesn't aspect the ascendant, which means that his placement is less fortunate that "normal" 5th house placements. So, when you are assessing a planet like that, you should say that "Neptune may be in the 5th house, but doesn't aspect the ascendant". If such a planet promised good fortune, this is greatly reduced by the lack of aspect with the ascendant.

Likewise, Jupiter may technically be in the 11th house, but he doesn't have the "normal" sextile relationship with the ascendant. I would personally consider him a 12th house planet in this case, as he is very close to the cusp. In any case, this is not a fortunate placement, 11th house or not. On the other hand, Mercury and the Moon, although placed in unfortunate houses, aspect the ascendant (the Moon is in the same sign as the ascendant and Mercury trines the ascendant) and this is fortunate.

Essential dignities and receptions

Using the Dorothean triplicity rulerships and the Egyptian terms, we have:

a) The Moon is in the domicile of Venus, in the exaltation of Saturn, in the triplicity of Saturn, in the terms of Saturn and in her own face. The Moon doesn't have much essential dignity (she is dignified only by face), but at least she is not peregrine (there is also a mutual reception with Saturn). The Moon is applying to both her rulers (Venus and Saturn) and so they both receive her. This is a positive testimony regardless of whether Venus and Saturn are significators or not. Venus is combust and this reception will not be particularly helpful to the Moon. The reception with Saturn is a very good one (although Saturn is cadent and retrograde) because it is not only single but mutual (Saturn is the Moon's face), the aspect is fortunate (a sextile) and if Saturn were a principal significator in the question, this would be one indication that shows perfection of the matter. There may be problems, because Saturn is a retrograde Infortune, but a testimony for yes, nonetheless.

b) Mars is in his own domicile, in the triplicity of Venus, in Saturn's terms and in Venus' face. There is no aspect between him and Venus, so there can be no reception, unless it is mutual, but there is no such reception. Even if there were a mutual reception, the absence of an aspect would have weakened it. The same goes for Saturn.

c) Saturn is in the domicile of Jupiter, in the triplicity of the Sun, in the terms of Venus and in the face of the Moon. He is not peregrine, because of the mutual receptions. We've already mentioned the mutual reception with the Moon (as far as mutual receptions go, it's not very strong, but it's a very strong single one) and there is a mutual reception with Venus as well. This reception is not particularly helpful, because the aspect is an opposition and Venus is combust. There is also a mutual reception with the Sun, but again, not a very strong one, because of the opposition and of the fact that triplicity is not the strongest of dignities. There is a single reception with Jupiter (with a separating aspect, though), but Jupiter is weak and in order to offset a square with an Infortune, you need more than that. However, this reception will not help Jupiter, but for Saturn this is not a problem.

d) Mercury is in his own domicile, in the triplicity of Saturn, in his own terms and in Jupiter's face. The reception with Jupiter is mutual and the aspect between them is applying (although probably hindered by Saturn, if this were a question). The single reception between Mercury and Saturn is not enough to offset an opposition with an Infortune in retrograde motion.

e) The Sun is in the domicile of Mercury, in the triplicity of Saturn, in the terms of Mars and in his own face. The Sun and Mars do not aspect each other and we've already talked about the mutual reception with Saturn. However, the reception with Mercury is the strongest single reception there is. A planet in his domicile receives all the planets found there, regardless of whether they are applying or separating, and he helps them a lot (the opposition with Saturn, however, is still a problem for all the Gemini planets).

f) Venus is in the domicile of Mercury, in the triplicity and terms of Saturn and the face of the Sun. We've already talked about her reception with Saturn. The fact that the Sun receives her by face is not enough to counterbalance the combustion. If this conjunction were in Leo or Aries, it would have been much better. Mercury receives her in his domicile and helps her, but the combustion is a serious problem.

g) Jupiter is in Mercury's domicile and exaltation, in the triplicity, terms and face of Venus. We've talked about the reception with Mercury and Venus could have offered some help (despite the separating aspect), but she is combust.

Accidental dignities

I don't fully agree with Lilly's point system for accidental dignity. Barbara offers her personal variation in her book and you may come up with your own. For example, in my opinion, the points Lilly gives for a planet free from the beams are extremely important for Mercury (who is always so close to the Sun) and, to a lesser extent, Venus, but not for the rest of the planets, because most of the time they are free from the beams. Anyway, in practice, we don't add up points, we are just interested in whether a planet is dignified or not, regardless of his actual points. Let's do some examples from the chart above (including essential dignities), following Lilly's point system:

a) The Moon: Lilly would put the Moon in the 12th house (using the whole sign house system, the Moon is in the 1st house), so she would get minus 5 points. She is slow, moving at 11°54' a day, so minus 2 points. How can we tell that a planet is slow, if we have no astrological software with this option? We set the date of the chart exactly a day later. If, for example, on the 24th of a month, Mercury is at 15° of a sign and 24 hours later, he is at 16°40', then Mercury moves at a speed of 1°40' a day. The average speed of Mercury is 1° per day approximately (you need to know the average speed of each planet), therefore Mercury is fast. In our example chart, the Moon is well below her average speed of 13°10'36" per day, so she is slow. Is our Moon increasing in light? Yes, and she gets 2 points. When the Moon is in signs after the one the Sun is in, until the degree exactly opposite him, in other words, when the Moon is moving away from the Sun (from New Moon to Full Moon), then she is increasing in light. After the Full Moon, the Moon is moving towards the Sun and she is decreasing in light. She is free from the beams and so she gets 5 points. Essential dignity: 1 point for face. No mutual receptions between domicile or exaltation. Total = 1 point.

b) Mars: 3 points for being in the 2nd house, –5 points for being retrograde, –2 points for being occidental (Put the Sun in the ascendant. All the planets that are above the horizon with the Sun in the ascendant are oriental, that is, they rose before the Sun. All the planets below the horizon are occidental. In our chart example, if we put the Sun in the ascendant, the 7th house cusp would be opposite the Sun, at 22°55' Sagittarius. So, all the planets in signs and degrees earlier than the degree of the Sun, up until its opposite degree are oriental, that is, Mercury, Uranus, Neptune and Pluto. Saturn, Mars, the Moon, Jupiter and Venus are occidental). Also, Mars gets 5 points for being free from the beams. Keep in mind that when a planet is retrograde, we don't care if he is swift or slow in motion. Finally, he gets 5 points for being in his domicile. Total score = 6 points.

c) Jupiter is conjunct the North Node, but the conjunction is not partill and according to Lilly, he doesn't get any points for that (I disagree). Jupiter is in the 12th house (I can't possibly view this Jupiter as an 11th house planet, although Lilly probably would), so he gets –5 points. He is fast (+2 points), he is occidental (–2 points), he is free from the beams (+5 points) and he is in his detriment (–5 points). Total score = –5 points.

Sect

The chart is diurnal (the Sun is above the horizon – the 1st/7th house axis), so it is the diurnal planets (Jupiter and Saturn, apart from the Sun of course) that rejoice. Jupiter is diurnally placed (where the Sun is), but in a nocturnal sign. Saturn is in a diurnal sign, but nocturnally placed.

As for nocturnal planets, Venus is completely out of sect (diurnally placed in a diurnal sign, in a diurnal chart) and so is the Moon. Mars is nocturnally placed in a nocturnal sign (although according to most traditional authors Mars prefers diurnal signs), but he cannot be in hayz because the chart itself is diurnal.

So how do we use sect? I would suggest that a significator in hayz is positive testimony whereas a planet completely out of sect is negative testimony. In natal charts, pay attention to the Fortunes and Infortunes. For diurnal charts, Jupiter is the Fortune of sect and therefore you can expect more benefit from him than Venus. The opposite is true for nocturnal charts.

Almutens

I don't agree with the view that the almuten of a chart should be the "best" planet in the chart. Lilly's method, in particular, allows for any planet to become almuten of the chart (if they have the right amount of essential and accidental dignity) regardless of whether this planet actually relates to the chart or not by having "power" over important places. The method Ibn Ezra presents in *The Book of Nativities and Revolutions* is much better in my opinion, because he aims to find the planet that has the most essential dignities in the most important places in a horoscope. Lilly's almuten may be completely disconnected from the rest of the chart, but Ibn Ezra's one is connected to the Lights, the ascendant, the prenatal lunation and the Lot of Fortune. However, Ibn Ezra also tries to find the "best" planet among the candidates by including accidental dignity, but personally I don't agree. In my opinion, the almuten of a chart should be calculated in the same way as the almuten of a house, which means only essential dignity (not of the planet itself, but in Ibn Ezra's important places) must be taken into account. In this way, the almuten of a chart can be in either good or bad condition itself and we can draw conclusions from that for the overall life of the native.

In horary astrology, I strongly recommend the use of the almutens and co–almutens of houses as co–rulers of the houses (along with the domicile rulers) using the Dorothean triplicity system and the Egyptian terms. If two (or three) planets score the same points at a particular degree on the cusp of the house, these are all co–almutens and I would suggest you use them all and not to try to make a choice between them (if they aspect the house etc.) As it will become evident in my example charts, the answer is quite often given by almutens and not by the commonly used domicile rulers. The problem with almutens of houses is that, with the exclusion of the angles, the rest of the house cusps change according to which house system the astrologer prefers.

One example from the above chart: The MC is at 19°11' in Cancer. The Moon gets five points as the domicile ruler, Jupiter gets four points as the exaltation ruler, Venus gets three points as the triplicity ruler, Jupiter gets two points as the term ruler and Mercury gets one point as the face ruler. Jupiter gets six points in total and therefore, he is the almuten of the MC.

Antiscia

As I've already said in the introduction, I have not found antiscia particularly useful in horary astrology (in the sense that you can reach the same conclusion without resorting to them), although there are astrologers who disagree.

Antiscia and contrantiscia are easy to calculate. Imagine a house wheel with Aries in the first house, Taurus in the second house, Gemini in the third house etc. The connection is as follows: the 1st sign has its antiscium in the 6th sign, so Aries has its antiscium in Virgo. The 2nd sign has its antiscium in the 5th (Taurus/Leo) and the 3rd sign with the 4th (Gemini/Cancer). We do the same thing with Libra as the first sign. Libra (1st sign) has its antiscium in the 6th sign (Pisces), Scorpio (2nd sign) in Aquarius (5th) and Sagittarius (3rd sign) in the 4th sign (Capricorn). Keep in mind that the degrees of the planet and the degrees of its antiscium must total 30. So a planet in the 3rd degree of Aries has its antiscium in the 27th degree of Virgo, a planet in the 14th degree of Gemini has its antiscium in the 16th degree of Cancer etc.

The contrantiscium of a planet is the degree opposite the one of its antiscium. So, in our previous examples, the contrantiscium of the 3rd degree of Aries is in the 27th degree of Pisces and the contrantsicium of the 14th degree of Gemini is in the 16th degree of Capricorn.

Planetary hour ruler

Planetary hours are not like clock hours, that is, they don't last sixty minutes and there is a difference between diurnal and nocturnal hours. Day begins at sunrise (Sun conjunct the ascendant) and ends at sunset (Sun conjunct the descendant). Night begins at sunset and lasts until the next sunrise. How long this lasts depends on the time of year and on the place the chart is cast. If, for example, daytime lasts 14 hours, then you have to divide 14 by 12 to find the correct length of the diurnal planetary hour, and for the nocturnal planetary hours, you have to divide 10 by 12.

The first hour is ruled by the planet that also rules the day in question. If the day is Tuesday, then the ruler of the day is Mars and, therefore, Mars also rules the first planetary hour. The next hour is ruled by the Sun, following the Chaldean order of the planets (Saturn, Jupiter, Mars, the Sun, Venus, Mercury, the Moon). The third hour is ruled by Venus and so on.

Calculation of the Lot of Fortune

I do not agree with Ptolemy and I reverse the formula for nocturnal charts. For the majority of the Lots, you start with the planet or Light in sect, so in this case, if the chart is nocturnal, you start with the Moon. I see no reason to make an exception for the Lot of Fortune and I have not heard a convincing argument to do this. In diurnal charts, you take the distance between the Sun and the Moon and cast from the ascendant and in nocturnal charts, you take the distance between the Moon and the Sun and cast it from the ascendant. In our example chart (diurnal), we start with the Sun and, following the order of signs, we seek the Moon. The Moon is approximately 103 degrees away from the Sun (7°05' in Gemini, 30° in Cancer, 30° in Leo, 30° in Virgo, and 5°53' in Libra) and if we cast this distance from the ascendant, we will reach 29° Capricorn.

Part Three
Example Charts
Second House Matters – Money

"Will We Agree on Payment?"
The querent was hoping he could work for a TV channel, but they seemed reluctant to pay him for his services since they thought the publicity they would provide was enough of a reward. The querent was expecting a proposition, but feared there would be no money involved.

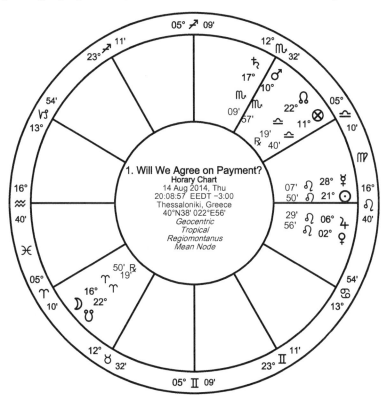

Querent: First house, Saturn (1st house domicile ruler and almuten), Jupiter (domicile ruler of the intercepted house in the 1st house), the Moon.

The Querent's money: Second house, Mars (domicile ruler of the 2nd house), the Sun (almuten of the 2nd house), the Moon, the South Node, Jupiter (natural ruler of wealth), the Lot of Fortune, Venus (domicile ruler of the Lot of Fortune), Saturn (almuten of the Lot of Fortune).

TV channel: Seventh house, the Sun (7th house domicile ruler and almuten), Mercury, possibly also Jupiter and Venus.

Testimonies for: The Moon is in the 2nd house of money. Jupiter and Venus, the two Fortunes, are conjunct in an angular sign and they have a mutual reception by terms. Mars and the Sun are in their domiciles. The Moon applies to the Sun with a trine and she is received. Mercury, though combust, is received by the Sun in his domicile. Saturn is received by Mars.

Testimonies against: The ruler of the 7th house in the 7th house is not usually good testimony for 7th house matters, as it indicates that the 7th house person stands by their own views and is not willing to compromise. Mercury, the ruler of the intercepted sign in the 7th house, is also in the 7th house. Mars, Venus, Mercury, the Sun and Jupiter are all afflicted by Saturn. Mars, principal significator of the querent's money, is applying to Saturn, an Infortune (Mars receives him, though). Even if we consider Mars a benefic here, Saturn most certainly isn't and the reception benefits Saturn, not Mars. The Lot of Fortune is in the 8th house (but trines the ascendant). The South Node in the 2nd house conjunct the Moon is a serious negative testimony.

Judgement: The Moon in the house of the matter enquired about establishes the radicality of the chart. The Sun/Moon applying trine is fortunate and implies that a proposition is indeed going to be made in five time units. However, the Sun in the 7th house shows unwillingness to compromise. Venus (significator of the money of the channel) applying to Jupiter (co–significator of the querent) is good testimony, but they are afflicted by Saturn. Similarly, Mars (money) applying to Saturn (querent and also almuten of the 8th house) could initially be considered a positive indication, because of them being significators, but it is a conjunction of the Infortunes and Mars is harmed by Saturn. The fact that the South Node is in the 2nd house, and that all the rulers of money are afflicted by Saturn, shows that either no money will be offered or the offer will not be to the querent's liking.

Outcome: A proposition (Sun/Moon trine) was indeed made almost five weeks later (minus two days). The querent said that he wanted money for his services and he hasn't heard from them since.

Astrological conclusions: The fact that Mars and Saturn are significators doesn't stop them from being Infortunes. In many 7th house matters, when the significators of the 7th house are in the house itself, this is not a good thing. The South Node in the house of the quesited is a major negative testimony.

"When Will She Pay Me?"

The querent had done some work for a friend of hers, but the friend hadn't paid her yet. She trusted the friend but she thought that the friend had probably forgotten.

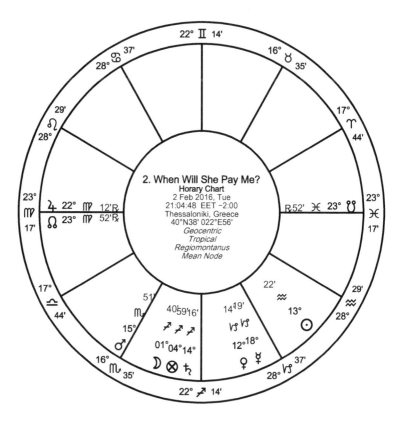

Querent: First house, Mercury (1st house domicile ruler and almuten), Jupiter, the Moon.

The Querent's money: Second house, Venus (domicile ruler of the 2nd house), Saturn (co–almuten of the 2nd house), Jupiter (natural ruler of wealth and ruler of the Lot of Fortune), the Lot of Fortune.

Friend: Eleventh house, the Moon (11th house domicile ruler and almuten).

Friend's money: Twelfth house and the Sun (12th house domicile ruler and almuten).

Testimonies for: There is an applying trine between Mercury (querent) and Jupiter (natural ruler of wealth and ruler of the Lot of Fortune) with reception. Mercury is free from combustion and the sunbeams, is increasing in speed and is conjunct Venus, the Fortune of sect. Mercury is also in a mutual reception with a dignified Mars. Jupiter, the other Fortune, is conjunct the ascendant and the North Node, which is also conjunct the ascendant. Venus is in Jupiter's terms and applies to trine Jupiter (also significator of the querent). There is a strong mutual reception between the Moon and Jupiter. The Moon is in the third house (but in the fourth sign from the ascendant), where she rejoices, and she's conjunct the Lot of Fortune. The Sun (the friend's money) applies to a sextile with Saturn (the querent's money) with a strong reception. The Moon applies to a sextile with the Sun (the friend's money), but the conjunction with Saturn will happen first (the querent's money) with a weak reception. Saturn may be an Infortune, but he is angular, in mutual reception with Venus and in single reception with the Sun. Venus is applying to a sextile with a dignified Mars and he receives her in his exaltation.

Testimonies against: Jupiter is in detriment, retrograde and square Saturn (although he receives him). The Sun is in detriment and doesn't aspect the ascendant. The Moon is afflicted by Saturn (although Saturn's condition is quite good and the aspect is out of orb at the moment of asking). The Sun makes a square with Mars (although Mars is practically a benefic here, being in his domicile and triplicity in a nocturnal chart and he is also in the Sun's face).

Judgement: This is quite a fortunate chart, with a lot of strong and positive testimonies. The querent will undoubtedly get her money (perhaps with some difficulty or it would require some action on her part). I couldn't be sure when that would happen exactly because of all those applying aspects. The Moon perfects the sextile with the Sun and the conjunction with Saturn in 13 degrees. Mercury perfects the trine with Jupiter in four degrees. The Sun perfects his sextile with Saturn in one degree. Venus perfects her trine with Jupiter in a little more than nine degrees (Jupiter is retrograde). Since the querent thought it was a matter of days (because she was determined to notify her friend if she didn't settle the matter soon), I told her that, on average, it will take a week more or less.

Outcome: The querent, not hearing from the friend, sent an email to her (Venus is applying to Mars, ruler of the 3rd house) exactly 9 days later and her friend said she had indeed forgotten, but she swore she had remembered it just before the querent's email and was amazed at the synchronicity. She promised that she would do it the next morning. The following morning (9 ½ days later – Venus/Jupiter trine perfection), the querent received her payment.

Astrological conclusions: The timing was given by Venus (querent's money) to Jupiter (co–significator of the querent). This is evidence that planets in houses are co–significators of the house, along with the domicile ruler and almuten of the house.

"Will the Restaurant Do Well?"

This was really a "should I?" question in the beginning. The querent wanted to know whether he should invest more money in the restaurant he had with a partner. I told him I don't believe in "should I?" questions and that astrology, in my opinion, doesn't give advice, so I could only look at the state of the business. He agreed, but radicality is doubtful. If the ruler of the hour (Saturn) harmonized with the ascendant, I would be happier, but he doesn't.

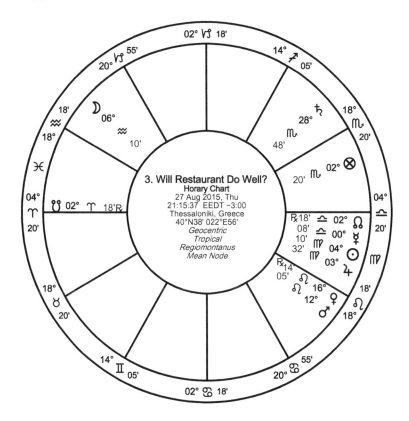

Querent: First house, Mars (1st house ruler and almuten), the Moon, the South Node.

The business: Tenth house, Saturn (domicile ruler and almuten of the 10th house), the Sun (natural significator of professional matters).

Querent's money: Second house, Venus (domicile ruler of the 2nd), the Moon (almuten of the 2nd house), Jupiter (natural significator of wealth), the Lot of Fortune, Mars (domicile ruler and almuten of the Lot of Fortune).

Partner: Seventh house, Venus (domicile ruler of the 7th house), Saturn (almuten of the 7th house).

Testimonies for: Mars is in the fortunate 5th house and trines the ascendant (normally, I would consider Mars to be in the 6th house, but in this case the natural 5th house with an Aries ascendant is Leo). The very swift–in–motion Moon trines angular Mercury (but separating) with a strong reception. Saturn (the restaurant and the partner) is in his own terms and in mutual reception with Mars (domicile, triplicity/terms). Mars and Venus, principal significators, are applying to conjunct each other.

Testimonies against: The South Node is conjunct the ascendant. Venus is retrograde and applies to conjunct Mars, an Infortune. Jupiter is combust, in detriment and in the 6th house. The Sun is in the 6th house. The Moon applies to an opposition with Mars without reception. Saturn is in the 8th house afflicting the partner's money. The Lot of Fortune is in the 8th house, in Scorpio. The Infortunes are principal significators.

Judgement: The positive testimonies are not strong at all. The Moon is separating from Mercury, Venus may be applying to a conjunction with Mars but she is retrograde, Mars is an Infortune and Saturn could be worse, but he is accidentally weak. On the other hand, the negative testimonies are very powerful. The South Node on the ascendant is very unfortunate and so is the Moon opposing Mars without reception. All the significators of the querent's money are very weak. Besides the Moon and retrograde Venus, Jupiter is combust, in detriment and in the 6th house. The mutually applying conjunction of Mars and Venus (either the querent and his partner or his money and the partner's money) may indicate that the querent will finally make the investment, but nothing good can come out of it. Moreover, Saturn (the business) will soon enter

Sagittarius, where he will be peregrine, so no actual improvement can be expected.

I told the querent that the restaurant is not going to do any better and even though I don't usually give advice to clients, I suggested he shouldn't invest.

Outcome: He invested more money. The situation wasn't improving and I found out later that his partnership with this person had cost him lots of money from previous investments. Five months later (the Moon's opposition with Mars perfects in a little less than six degrees, but the Moon is very fast and it speeded up the process), the querent decided to leave the partnership, apparently with no big loss this time around.

"When Will He Pay Me?"

The Querent was expecting some money for a job (partnership) he had done and he was promised they would pay him the day before the question, but that didn't happen.

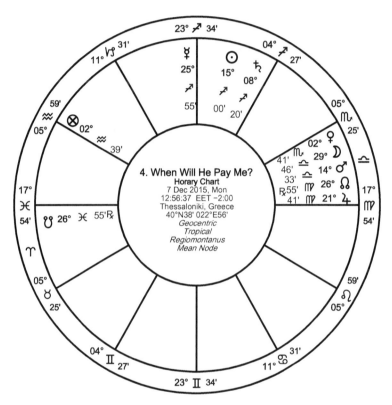

4. When Will He Pay Me?
Horary Chart
7 Dec 2015, Mon
12:56:37 EET −2:00
Thessaloniki, Greece
40°N38' 022°E56'
Geocentric
Tropical
Regiomontanus
Mean Node

The Moon is technically void in course, but at the very end of her void course and it is debatable whether she was ever really void in course, given the fact that her previous aspect with Mercury is very close and she is about to change sign and immediately apply to another planet.

Querent: First house, Jupiter (domicile ruler of the 1st house), Venus (almuten of the 1st house), the Moon, the South Node, Mars (domicile ruler of the intercepted sign in the 1st house).

Querent's money: Second house, Venus (domicile ruler and almuten of the 2nd house), Jupiter (natural significator of wealth), the Lot of Fortune, Saturn (domicile ruler and almuten of the Lot of Fortune).

Partner: Seventh house, Mercury (domicile ruler and almuten of the 7th house), Jupiter, the Moon, Mars, the North Node.

Testimonies for: The Moon applies to Venus (both the querent and his money) with reception (Venus receives the Moon in her domicile and after the change of sign, she will receive the Moon in her triplicity). Saturn (ruler of the Lot of Fortune) is about to leave combustion and he is received by the Sun in his triplicity. Mercury is angular, free from combustion (but still under the beams) and received by the Sun in his triplicity. Venus has a strong mutual reception with Mars (no aspect, though). Jupiter is angular, conjunct the North Node and in strong mutual reception with Mercury. Jupiter also has a mutual reception with Mars between terms. The Moon is in fact translating light from Mercury (debtor) to Venus (querent and his money).

Testimonies against: The South Node is in the 1st house. The Lot of Fortune is in the 12th house. Jupiter, Mercury, Mars and Venus are in detriment. The aspects between Mercury and the Moon and between Mercury and Jupiter are squares. The Moon is in the Via Combusta.

Judgement: Venus, the almuten of the 1st house, conjunct the 8th house cusp shows that the querent is interested in the money of his partner and establishes radicality of the chart. There is hardly any essential dignity, but the mutual receptions help a lot. Venus is a Fortune in her triplicity and the Moon/Venus mutually applying conjunction with reception is enough of a testimony to bring the matter to conclusion. The aspect will perfect in 3°14' minutes, but the Moon is painfully slow.

Outcome: The querent told me he contacted the people responsible in three hours and 45 minutes and they apologized to him for the delay. Four hours after the question, he received payment.

Astrological conclusions: Essential debility and hard aspects are not such a problem when the Fortunes are involved and there is strong mutual reception or a single reception between two planets in conjunction. Had emphasis been put on the fact that Venus is in the sign of the Moon's fall, it would have given a wrong answer.

"When Will the Money Arrive?"

The querent was expecting some money from abroad, via internet banking. This usually takes two or three days, but more days had passed and the querent wanted to know when the amount would appear in his bank account.

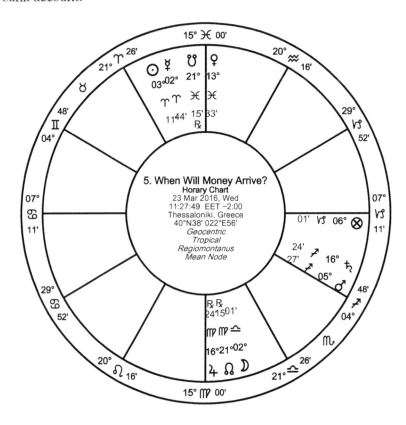

Querent: First house, the Moon (1st house domicile ruler), Venus (1st house almuten).

Querent's money: Second house, the Moon (2nd house domicile ruler and almuten), probably the Sun, who has more degrees in the 2nd house than Cancer and Leo is the natural second house sign with a Cancer ascendant, Jupiter (natural ruler of wealth), the Lot of Fortune, Saturn (domicile ruler and almuten of the Lot of Fortune).

Other people's money: Eighth house, Saturn (8th house domicile ruler), Mars (8th house almuten).

Testimonies for: The two Fortunes are angular (although they oppose each other) and Venus, almuten of the ascendant, is also in the sign of her exaltation and triplicity. The Moon applies to a sextile with Mars and Saturn (other people's money) and there is mutual reception. The Sun is in the sign of his exaltation. Jupiter is conjunct the North Node. The Moon is in her own face. The Lot of Fortune is angular. The Sun (co–significator of the querent's money) applies to a trine with Mars (8th house almuten) with a strong reception. Venus and Jupiter have a mutual reception.

Testimonies against: Mars and Saturn, the two Infortunes, are significators of the other person's money and they are in the 6th house, not aspecting the ascendant and conjunct each other without reception, therefore afflicting one another. Venus is conjunct the South Node and afflicted by both the Infortunes. The sextiles of the Moon with Mars and Saturn are hindered by the Moon's opposition with Mercury and the opposition with the Sun without reception. Jupiter makes a partill square with Saturn (with a single reception which is not enough to counterbalance a square with an Infortune).

Judgement: The problem, it seems, is not when, but whether the money will actually arrive or not. The sextiles the Moon is about to make are severely hindered by her oppositions with Mercury and especially the Sun, which is a very negative testimony. Venus applies to oppose Jupiter with mutual reception (but an opposition nonetheless) while at the same time she will make a partill square with Saturn, an Infortune. Things don't look good and there is strong possibility that no money will arrive because of some kind of problem. Because of the applying sextiles of the Moon, the applying trine of the Sun to Mars and Venus' essential and accidental strength, the querent will get his money in the end, but a new transaction probably has to take place.

Outcome: The money never came. The querent informed the other person who confirmed that something went wrong with the bank transaction and the money was returned to him. The querent received the money via a third person a little less than four weeks later (the Moon perfects the aspect with Mars in 3½ degrees, but she is very slow and it will take longer. The Sun needs three degrees to perfect the trine with Mars).

Astrological conclusions: A hard aspect between the Lights is always a problem. Here, Mercury and the Sun hinder the Moon/Mars sextile because the aspect is an opposition and there is no reception. The timing of the final payment was given by the aspects to the almuten (Mars) and not the domicile ruler (Saturn).

Part Four
Example charts
Seventh House Matters – Relationships

"How Will Things Go?"

The querent was in a relationship with a woman from abroad and things weren't going very well. She was being very distant and cold towards him. He was going to meet her in her country and was wondering if things would straighten out.

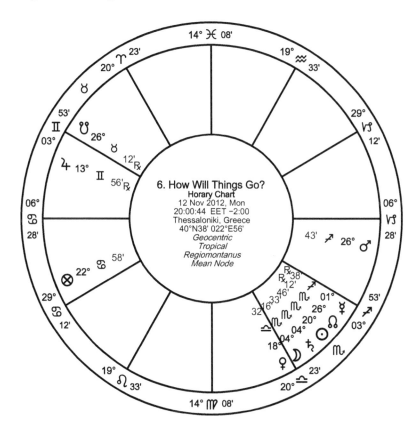

Querent: First house, the Moon (1st house domicile ruler and co–almuten), Mars (1st house co–almuten).

Girlfriend: Seventh house, Saturn (7th house ruler and almuten).

Testimonies for: Both principal significators (the Moon, Saturn) are in the fortunate 5th house and trine the ascendant. The Lot of Fortune is in the 1st house. Mars rejoices in the 6th house and is in his terms. There is a weak mutual reception between Mars and Jupiter (they oppose each other, though, and Jupiter is very weak). Saturn is about to move away from the sunbeams.

Testimonies against: The Moon is in the sign of her fall and makes a partill conjunction with the Infortune out of sect, a peregrine Saturn. Mars may rejoice in the 6th house, but he is cadent and doesn't aspect the ascendant. The Moon is already under the sunbeams and moves into combustion. She is also in the Via Combusta.

Judgement: The Moon is greatly afflicted by both Saturn and the Sun. The Moon and Saturn have no reception and nothing good can come out of a conjunction like this one. The fact that they are in a partill conjunction shows their imminent encounter, but the querent should definitely keep his hopes low.

Outcome: It was very bad. She was distant the whole time he was there. Sometime later, she came to Greece and it was the last time they met. They broke up soon afterwards (the Moon is moving towards combustion).

Astrological conclusions: Once more, the Infortunes never stop being Infortunes, regardless of whether they are significators or not. The same goes for the Sun. When the Sun is a significator, he can still "burn" a planet by conjuncting it.

"Will I Get a Divorce?"

The querent was in a troubled marriage for many years, but a divorce never materialized, because his wife wouldn't hear of it. When he found out that she was seeing another man, he wanted to get out of the marriage as soon as possible.

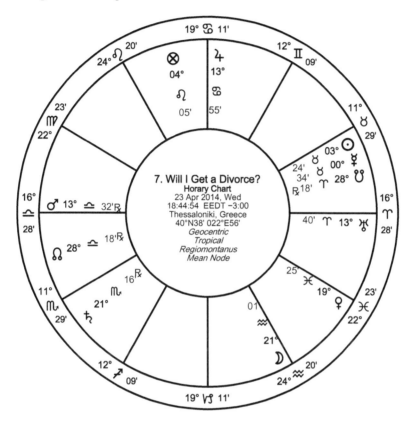

Querent: First house, Venus (1st house domicile ruler), Saturn (1st house almuten), Mars, the Moon, the North Node.

Wife: Seventh house, Mars (7th house domicile ruler), the Sun (7th house almuten), the South Node.

Testimonies for: Venus is exalted and she has a mutual reception with an angular exalted Jupiter. Mars is in mutual reception with Saturn (no aspect, though, and Mars is severely debilitated while Saturn is retrograde and doesn't aspect the ascendant). The Sun applies to sextile Jupiter.

Testimonies against: The South Node is in the house of marriage. Venus is in the 6th house and doesn't aspect the ascendant. Mars, the planet of disharmony and rupture, is conjunct the ascendant. Mars is also in detriment and retrograde. The Moon is in a partill square with Saturn (with reception though). Jupiter is afflicted by his partill square with Mars. I do not normally use outer planets in horary work, but Uranus, a planet that has very little to do with Aquarius but a lot to do with Mars, is conjunct the descendant and makes a partill opposition with Mars, intensifying the theme of rupture. The Sun in the 8th house will eventually oppose Saturn (although the aspect is out of orb at the moment of the question). If you are fond of antiscia, Mars (rupture) applies to conjunct Venus' antiscium (querent).

Judgement: Mars on the ascendant is a clear sign of divorce or separation at least (although being the 7th house ruler, this is also an indication that the wife doesn't want it). There may be a reception between the Moon and Saturn, but to take away the malice of a square with an Infortune, you would need a strong mutual reception and even then problems may still arise. The Sun and Saturn are in opposing signs and opposition is the aspect of "separate ways" and complete disagreement. The Lot of Marriage in horary charts (Asc + Desc – Venus), according to Al Biruni, is at 13° Scorpio, afflicted by Saturn and has this debilitated Mars as its ruler (Jupiter trines it, though). The positive testimonies are not enough to outweigh the strong negative ones. The couple will separate.

Outcome: Four months and a week later, the querent's wife moved out and they separated, but they didn't get a divorce (Jupiter makes a partill trine to the Lot of Marriage). The Sun needs approximately 16½ degrees (weeks, as it turned out) to perfect the opposition with Saturn.

Astrological conclusions: The Sun and Mercury have an 8th house relationship with the ascendant. Even if one considers them to be in the 7th house, they cannot be 7th house significators, because they are in a different sign from the one in the cusp. Uranus in the 1st/7th house axis in relationship charts is not a good testimony. A square with an Infortune needs a very strong mutual reception for it to stop being such a problem. The timing of the separation was shown by the opposition of the almutens and not by the domicile rulers.

"Will There Be a Relationship?"

The querent was fed up chasing a man, who showed some interest, but nothing significant had happened until the time of the question. She was ready to give up.

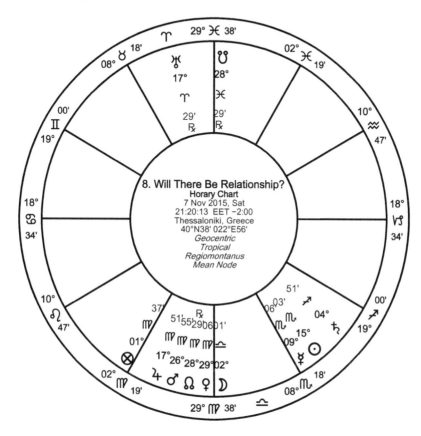

Querent: First house, the Moon (1st house domicile ruler and almuten).

Potential boyfriend: Seventh house, Saturn (7th house domicile ruler and co–almuten), Mars (7th house co–almuten).

Testimonies for: The Moon is applying to Saturn with a sextile and she is received in his exaltation. Mars makes a conjunction with the North Node and with both Fortunes (enclosure). The Moon and Venus have a mutual reception (no aspect). Mars has a very strong mutual reception with Mercury.

Testimonies against: Saturn is in the 6th sign from the ascendant and doesn't aspect it.

Judgement: The applying sextile of the Moon with Saturn with such strong reception leaves us with no doubt that something positive will happen in almost three time units, although the Moon is very slow and this may take longer. The potential boyfriend is in the turned 12th house, which may indicate that the boyfriend has some personal/psychological issues to deal with. The Moon is angular and in a moveable sign, so months seem unlikely, probably weeks or days.

Outcome: The querent was greatly surprised with what I told her, because she was ready to forget all about it. Four days later, however, they started a relationship, which had its ups and downs. The boyfriend had recently lost both of his parents and he was in a troubled marriage.

Astrological conclusions: A single reception is very effective when we have an applying fortunate aspect. A relationship did happen. The fact that Saturn is indifferent towards the Moon may indicate that this relationship won't last very long or there may be other problems, but if you place too much emphasis on this, you will miss the actual fact, that a relationship did form.

"Will We Get Back Together?"

The querent had broken up with a woman many years younger than him and he was anxious to know whether they would get back together.

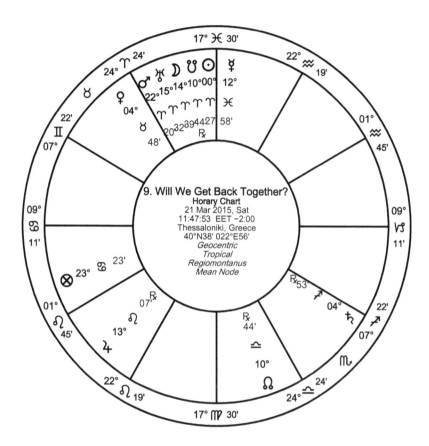

9. Will We Get Back Together?
Horary Chart
21 Mar 2015, Sat
11:47:53 EET −2:00
Thessaloniki, Greece
40°N38' 022°E56'
Geocentric
Tropical
Regiomontanus
Mean Node

Querent: First house, The Moon (1st house domicile ruler), Venus (1st house almuten).

Girlfriend: Seventh house, Saturn (7th house domicile ruler and almuten).

Testimonies for: Venus is in domicile in the fortunate 11th house. The Moon has left combustion, which, in any case, was less damaging than usual because of the strong reception. The Moon is applying to Mars, who receives her in his domicile. The Moon makes a (separating) trine with Jupiter, a Fortune. The Lot of Fortune is in the 1st house. The Sun applies to a trine with Saturn with reception.

Testimonies against: Saturn is retrograde in the 6th house. The Moon is conjunct the South Node and Uranus (see previous charts) and she is still under the beams. The Moon is separating from Saturn and Venus doesn't aspect Saturn. Venus is applying to a square without reception with retrograde Jupiter, who doesn't aspect the ascendant.

Judgement: This is not an unfortunate chart in general. However, despite the dignities and receptions, the fact that there aren't any applying aspects between our significators is very unfortunate for the querent. The applying conjunction between the Moon and Mars may be beneficial to the Moon in general because of the reception, but Mars is an enemy of relationships. The conjunction of the Moon to Uranus doesn't help either. However, the essential dignities of the significators of the querent indicate that even if they don't get back together, this is going to be good for the querent. Also, the Sun (natural significator of men) applying to trine Saturn may show a new relationship for the young woman.

Outcome: They did not get back together.

Astrological conclusions: In "Will we get back together?" charts, an applying aspect between the significators seems necessary and an overall good fortune is not enough. The Sun should not be given to the man of the question, because he can signify a third person. Once again, Uranus seems to play a negative role in relationship charts.

"Will Things Get Better?"

The querent was in a relationship with a woman that wasn't going well. He wanted to know if the situation would improve.

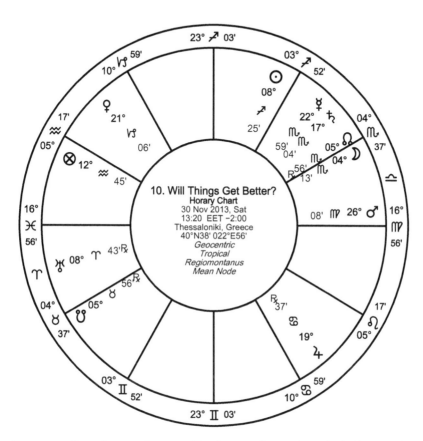

Querent: First house, Jupiter (1st house domicile ruler), Venus (1st house almuten), Mars (domicile ruler of the intercepted sign in the 1st house), the Moon.

Girlfriend: Seventh house, Mercury (7th house domicile ruler and almuten), Mars.

Testimonies for: Venus is in the fortunate 11th house in her triplicity and terms. She makes a trine with Mars with mutual reception (exaltation/triplicity) and a sextile with Saturn with mutual reception (domicile/

triplicity). Jupiter is in the fortunate 5th house and he is exalted. The Moon is conjunct the North Node.

Testimonies against: The Moon is in fall in the 8th house and applies to conjunct Saturn, an Infortune in the 8th house without reception. Mars, the planet of rupture, is in the seventh house of relationships. The sextile between the Moon and Venus is hindered by Saturn. The trine between Venus and Mars will never perfect as Venus is slowing down. Mercury has separated from Venus and he has also separated from Jupiter and Mars. Jupiter is retrograde. The Moon is in the Via Combusta. Uranus is in the intercepted sign in the 1st house.

Judgement: Mars on the descendant (although in this case, being one of the querent's significators, it also shows that the querent is very much interested in maintaining the relationship), is a very clear sign of separation. There are no applying aspects between the significators and the Moon's conjunction with Saturn in the 8th house is very unfortunate.

Outcome: They separated shortly afterwards.

Astrological conclusions: Mars in the 7th house in relationship charts is a very negative indication as Barbara Dunn clearly showed in several chart examples in her book. A conjunction with an Infortune without reception will almost always destroy the matter. Again, Uranus in the 1st/7th house axis in relationship charts plays a negative role.

"Will There Be a Relationship Between Us?"

The querent had met a colleague of hers from another country that she fancied and she believed he showed interest.

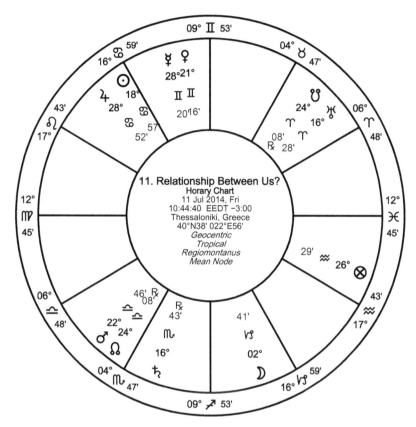

Querent: First house, Mercury (1st house domicile ruler and almuten), the Moon.

Potential boyfriend: Seventh house, Jupiter (7th house domicile ruler and almuten).

Testimonies for: Mercury is in his domicile, angular and free from the beams. He is slow in motion but increasing in speed. He is also conjunct Venus, a Fortune. Jupiter is in his exaltation, in the fortunate 11th house, which is also the house of his joy. The Moon next applies to Saturn, her dispositor (we have reception therefore), with a sextile. Venus next applies to a trine with Mars, with reception.

Testimonies against: The Moon is in detriment and her aspect with Saturn is out of orb. Jupiter is under the beams and moves into combustion soon. Mercury will pick up speed, change sign and move under the beams. Mercury and Jupiter don't aspect each other. The Moon will eventually oppose Jupiter with reception, but first she will oppose the Sun (there is reception, but an opposition of the Lights is always serious) and if that wasn't enough, she will square Mars in detriment (there is also reception here, but the reception is not mutual and they are both in detriment). All the Moon aspects though, are out of orb at the moment of the question.

Judgement: There are fortunate testimonies, but the lack of an aspect between the main significators and the fact that both of them are threatened or about to be threatened by the Sun indicate that there isn't going to be a relationship. The Moon will eventually aspect Jupiter, but first she will make hard aspects with the Sun and Mars. Anyway, the opposition with Jupiter, even if it were the Moon's next aspect and within orb, makes it doubtful that something satisfactory or lasting would happen.

Outcome: A relationship never happened.

Astrological conclusions: The lack of an aspect again proves crucial. The main significators may be essentially dignified but they are or will be afflicted by the Sun, which is serious.

"Will They Divorce?"

The querent was the best man at a friend's wedding, but things weren't going well and he was wondering whether the marriage would end.

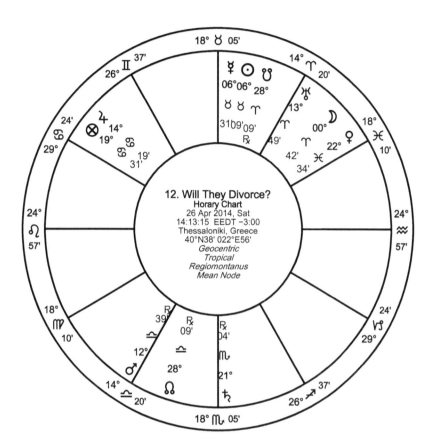

Friend: Eleventh house, Mercury (11th house domicile ruler and co–almuten), Saturn (11th house co–almuten).

Friend's husband: Fifth house, Jupiter (5th house domicile ruler and almuten).

Marriage: The Lot of Marriage in horary charts (distance from Venus to the cusp of the 7th house and cast from the ascendant) is at 27°21' Cancer, so the Moon is the domicile ruler and almuten.

This is a third person chart for a relationship and, according to Barbara Dunn, signification must also be taken from the unturned chart, the radical 1st/7th house axis. So, the Sun (1st house domicile ruler and almuten), Saturn (7th house domicile ruler and almuten) and, naturally, the Moon.

Testimonies for: Jupiter is exalted. The Sun has a mutual reception with the Moon. Saturn makes a (separating) trine with Venus with reception. Mercury applies to Jupiter with a sextile. The Sun and Mercury are in the angular 10th sign from the ascendant (from the 9th house side). The Sun applies to sextile Jupiter. Mars and Saturn are in mutual reception. Venus and Jupiter have a mutual reception.

Testimonies against: Jupiter doesn't aspect the ascendant and is afflicted by retrograde Mars in detriment. Mercury is combust and the sextile with Jupiter will perfect while he is still combust. The Moon's next aspect is an opposition with retrograde Mars in detriment, the planet of rupture (with reception though), and immediately after that, she will conjunct Uranus. The sextile between the Sun and Jupiter (even if we don't consider Mercury to be a prohibiting factor) is going to happen while they are both afflicted, Jupiter by Mars and the Sun by Saturn. The Sun will oppose Saturn (after the sextile with Jupiter). Saturn, an Infortune, is retrograde and by being angular casts a shadow over the whole chart.

Judgement: The applying aspects between the main significators are not very promising. It is doubtful whether a combust planet can ever bring a successful outcome. The Sun will also sextile Jupiter, but they are both afflicted by the two Infortunes. The mutual reception between Mars and Saturn cannot be of much help to either of them, since there is no aspect, they are not essentially dignified and they are both retrograde. The Moon's opposition to Mars, despite the reception, is not positive given the condition of Mars and the nature of the aspect.

Outcome: Approximately ten months later, she met a therapist who helped her with her issues (the Sun's sextile to Jupiter needs nine and a half degrees to perfect while the Sun is slow in motion) and this experience prompted her to file for a divorce a year later (5 May

2015 – the Moon's opposition to Mars). The divorce became final on 7 July 2015, fourteen and a half months later (the Sun will perfect the opposition with Saturn in 14 degrees).

Astrological conclusions: The unturned chart works better and also provides us with the correct timing.

"Will I Find Someone?"

The querent's marriage, while it lasted, was not particularly happy. The husband had now died and she was wondering if she would ever have a loving relationship with someone.

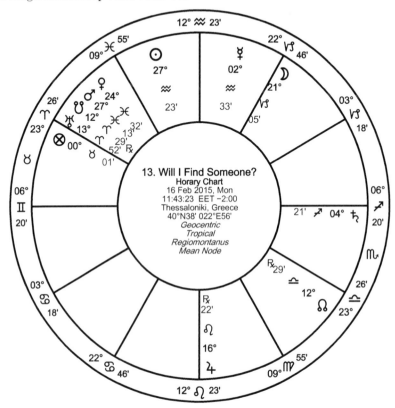

Querent: First house, Mercury (1st house domicile ruler and almuten), the Moon.

Possible new partner: Seventh house, Jupiter (7th house domicile ruler and almuten), Saturn.

Testimonies for: The Moon is swift in motion and applies to an exalted Venus with reception. The Moon also applies to Mars (though he is the planet of rupture) who receives her in his exaltation. Mars is in his own terms and face and received by Venus. Mercury applies to sextile Saturn in the 7th house with strong reception. Mercury and Jupiter are in angular signs. Mercury is in his own terms and Venus is also in her triplicity. Jupiter is in his face and in mutual reception with Saturn (terms/domicile).

Testimonies against: Saturn afflicts the 7th house. Mercury is very slow (but increasing in speed). Jupiter is retrograde. The Moon is in detriment and doesn't aspect the ascendant. Mercury applies to an opposition with Jupiter without reception.

Judgement: The Mercury/Jupiter opposition is not fortunate, but there are two very fortunate testimonies, the sextile between the Moon and Venus (a harmonious aspect between the Moon and Venus is always a positive indication in relationship charts) and the sextile between Mercury and Saturn. It seems that there is going to be a relationship. However, the opposition between Mercury and Jupiter is not very promising and Saturn afflicting the 7th house by his presence will certainly cause problems. The sextile between Mercury and Saturn will perfect in two degrees, the sextile between the Moon and Venus in 3.5 degrees and the Mercury/Jupiter opposition in 12 degrees.

Outcome: A relationship (with problems) indeed took place eight months later. The timing seems quite off. The Mercury/Jupiter opposition seems closer in time. The process was perhaps speeded up because of the angularity of the planets involved, their mutual applying and the fact that Jupiter is retrograde (indicating a sudden event). Interestingly, the querent is a very "saturnian" person with the Moon conjunct Saturn in Capricorn in the Midheaven and the person she fell in love with has the ruler of the ascendant and the Sun opposite Saturn in Capricorn. Saturn in the 7th house in the horary chart seems to describe the situation very well.

Astrological conclusions: A harmonious aspect between the Moon and Venus is more than welcome in relationship charts. Once again, the fact that Saturn "hates" Mercury may indicate that there may be problems in the relationship, but had you put emphasis on this and ignored the true reception between Mercury and Saturn, it would have led you to the wrong conclusion. The relationship had – and still has – some problems, but almost two years later, they are still together.

"Is It Over? Will We Be Together Again?"

The querent was having an affair with a married man. She wasn't interested in a relationship, she simply wanted them to be together and meet sporadically, whenever possible. He, on the other hand, wanted the affair to be over and he offered his friendship instead. The querent wasn't sure that he meant it, because he wasn't at all reliable.

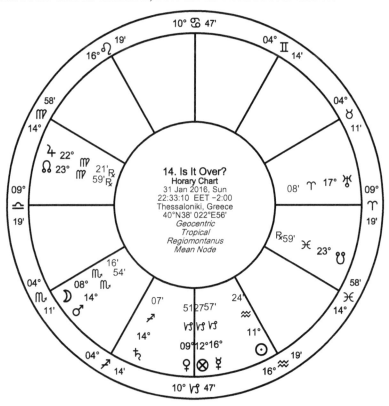

Querent: First house, Venus (1st house domicile ruler and almuten), the Moon.

Boyfriend: Seventh house, Mars (7th house domicile ruler and almuten).

Testimonies for: The Moon's first aspect is a sextile with Venus with mutual reception (the Moon is in Venus' terms and Venus is in the triplicity of the Moon). Venus is angular. The Moon is also applying to conjunct Mars (boyfriend) and Mars receives her in his domicile. Venus is applying to a sextile with Mars with reception.

Testimonies against: The Moon is in fall, in the Via Combusta and doesn't aspect the ascendant. After the sextile with Venus, the Moon will square the Sun without reception, which comes before the Moon/Mars conjunction. The Sun is applying to square Mars with a very weak single reception (face) and prohibits the sextile between Venus and Mars (although they happen almost simultaneously). Uranus is in the 7th house. The ascendant is closely conjunct the fixed star Vindemiatrix, often connected with widowhood, therefore not favourable for relationships.

Judgement: The only positive indication is the sextile between the Moon and Venus, which indicates some form of contact between them and that all is not quite over yet. However, the Moon/Mars conjunction is prohibited by the Sun (although this is not technically a prohibition) and the Venus/Mars sextile is also prohibited by the Sun. The Sun is the ruler of the 11th house and posited in the 5th house. Could it be that he is thinking of his child? Or is it that he only sees her as a friend? Whatever it is, what the querent has in mind cannot happen. She can expect something positive initially, but nothing good can come out of it.

Outcome: After a couple of weeks she contacted him and they communicated by phone (almost every day for a week or so) as if nothing had happened, although he showed no signs of wanting to resume the affair. He also confessed to some health problems. After that, the communication ended and four months after the question, he contacted her again, as a friend, and asked her why she hadn't tried to communicate with him all this time. She explained to him that she did not want his friendship, but she wanted them to be together as a couple. He refused and promised to not bother her again. He resurfaced, though, and they had a couple of telephone conversations. No real relationship has formed so far, however, and the querent doubts it ever will.

Astrological conclusions: This is a very good chart to show the concept of prohibition. In two cases, the aspects that would possibly show a positive outcome were hindered by squares with no or very weak receptions. Uranus, again, in the 7th house of relationships is a negative indication in relationship charts.

"Is There a Future in My Relationship?"

The querent was pregnant, but her boyfriend had left to work in another country. He told her there was no way he would stay in Greece and that the only way they could be together was for her to leave as well. She was reluctant to do that, though, because her job and family were in Greece.

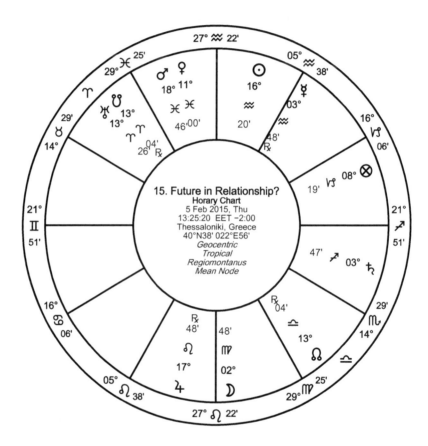

Querent: First house, Mercury (1st house domicile ruler and almuten), the Moon.

Boyfriend: Seventh house, Jupiter (7th house domicile ruler and almuten), Saturn (possibly).

Baby: Fifth house, Venus (domicile ruler of the interrupted sign in the 5th house and also domicile ruler of the Lot of Children at 7°50' Libra, taken, in diurnal charts, from the distance between Jupiter and Saturn and cast from the ascendant), Mercury (domicile ruler and almuten of the sign on the 5th house cusp), Saturn (almuten of the Lot of Children).

Testimonies for: Mercury applies to a sextile with Saturn with a strong reception. Venus is strongly dignified. Jupiter and Saturn have a mutual reception. The North Node is in the 5th house (baby). The Sun and Saturn have a mutual reception. Mercury is in his own terms.

Testimonies against: Venus is besieged by the two Infortunes (the Moon, though, will oppose Venus before her conjunction with Mars). Mercury and Jupiter, the two principal significators, are retrograde. Jupiter is opposite the Sun (the Sun receives him, though) and Mercury is still under the beams. After Mercury turns direct, he will oppose Jupiter. The Moon applies to an opposition with Venus (with reception, though), but first and most importantly, she will square Saturn without reception.

Judgement: Mercury will sextile Saturn twice (once retrograde and once direct) and this is positive, but Mercury is weak at the moment of asking, by being retrograde, cadent and under the beams. His situation will improve, but when he sextiles Saturn again, he is still going to be very slow. Jupiter is in a bad state by being retrograde and afflicted by the opposition with the Sun, despite the reception. The baby may seem strong, with Venus being dignified and with the North Node in the 5th house, but she is besieged by the two Infortunes. The Moon will oppose Venus (with reception, though) and Venus is also the ruler of the baby's 8th house. Mercury, after the sextile with Saturn, will oppose retrograde Jupiter and if we consider Saturn a 7th house planet, he afflicts the 7th house by his presence. The testimonies seem mixed so far. They are not very fortunate, but they could be much worse. However, the applying square of the Moon with Saturn without reception leaves us with no doubt. There can be no future with this configuration, combined with the rest of the testimonies. I told her that even if she decided to go with him, she would regret it after a while as there was no future in the stars for them.

Outcome: I heard from her more than a year later. She didn't go with her boyfriend and she didn't keep the baby.

Astrological conclusions: This chart stresses the importance of the Moon in every horary chart. Even very fortunate testimonies in a chart cannot easily overcome a Moon/Saturn square without reception.

"Will There Be a Relationship?"

The querent was having telephone conversations with a man and it seemed that he showed interest.

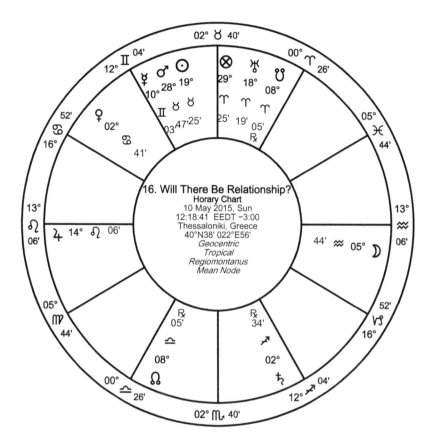

Querent: First house, the Sun (1st house domicile ruler and almuten), Jupiter, the Moon.

Love interest: Seventh house, Saturn (7th house domicile ruler and almuten), the Moon.

Testimonies for: Jupiter, the Fortune of sect, is on the ascendant. The Moon's next aspect is a trine with Mercury in domicile. The Sun and the Moon are angular. Jupiter is in his own face and in mutual reception (with a separating aspect) with Saturn.

Testimonies against: The Moon is separating from Saturn (with reception though). Saturn is retrograde. The Sun and Saturn do not aspect each other. The Moon, after the trine with Mercury, will next oppose Jupiter (with reception by terms at the time of the opposition, though) and square the Sun, a principal significator (also with reception). Mars, the planet of rupture, and Saturn are mutually applying to oppose each other (after Mars changes sign). The Sun is also separating from Jupiter and is afflicted by the conjunction with Mars in detriment.

Judgement: This is not a very clear chart. Naturally, unafflicted Jupiter on the ascendant is a positive indication in every chart and the Moon applying to Mercury is also fortunate. The applying aspects between the significators, however, are a square and an opposition with single receptions, but we need strong mutual receptions for such configurations. This is not an unfortunate, but neither a fortunate chart. Something could happen between them (although I wasn't even expecting that), but as I told the querent, nothing important or anything that would last.

Outcome: According to the querent, a relationship did happen around August, three months later or thereabouts. She seemed satisfied with it in the beginning, but the man in question had problems. He had a child that died, which deeply affected him, and he wanted to have children more than anything else. The querent however, was not at a reproductive age and even if she could have children, she didn't want to, as she already has two of her own. Problems started to arise and a few months later, they broke up. It was the querent who wanted out, because she "was tired of all this".

Astrological conclusions: An opposition, even with a Fortune, is never a desirable thing. Lilly was right in saying that the matter perfected with an opposition doesn't last very long. Also, this chart shows that planets in houses and not just the domicile rulers and almutens, should also be considered as significators.

"Will We Get Back Together?"

The querent was married, but he and his wife had separated. He wanted to know whether they would get back together.

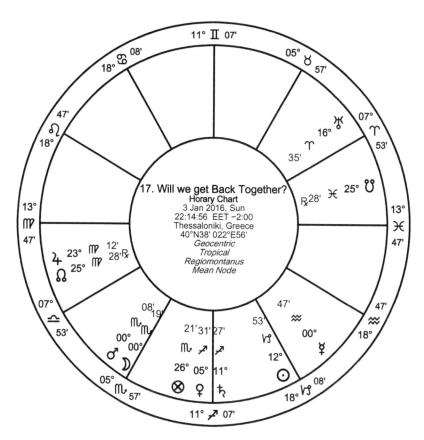

Querent: First house, Mercury (1st house domicile ruler and almuten), Jupiter, the Moon.

Wife: Seventh house, Jupiter (7th house domicile ruler and almuten).

Testimonies for: Jupiter, the 7th house domicile ruler and almuten, is in the first house. The Moon is exactly conjunct Mars, her dispositor by domicile, triplicity, terms and face and, therefore, he strongly receives her. Mercury is in his triplicity and terms. The Moon applies to sextile the Sun. Mercury will trine Jupiter (but after turning retrograde).

Testimonies against: The Moon applies to square Mercury without reception. Mercury is about to turn retrograde and will again perfect the square with Mars without reception. Mars is the planet of rupture and even though he is dignified here, it's best if he is out of the picture. Jupiter will also turn retrograde and the trine between him and Mercury will perfect when they are both retrograde. Even so, Mercury will square Mars first without reception. A square without reception is a clear negative testimony. The South Node is in the 7th house of relationships. The Sun will trine Jupiter before Mercury can reach him and although not a prohibition (there will also be a weak reception when the aspect perfects), this may be an indication that the wife (Jupiter) may meet somebody else (Sun). Venus, natural ruler of relationships, applies to conjunct angular Saturn. The Moon is in fall and in the Via Combusta.

Judgement: The square between the Moon and Mercury is without reception, which is a problem. The trine between the two significators, despite the reception, is not promising because they will both be retrograde. Even if they get back together, things will fall apart again. However, the fact that even this (problematic) trine is hindered by a square with Mars, makes it almost certain that they won't get back together.

Outcome: They did not get back together. In January 2017, the querent asked for a divorce.

Astrological conclusions: Even in questions like "Will we get back together?" we still want an applying aspect between direct planets and it's unsafe to view this literally ("they will go back to one another, because they move backwards"). Also, a square aspect that intervenes without reception is almost always a hindrance.

Part Five
Example Charts
Tenth House Matters – Career and Achievement

"Will I Have to Close Down the Shop?"

The querent was going through some rough times regarding her clothes shop and she felt the end was imminent.

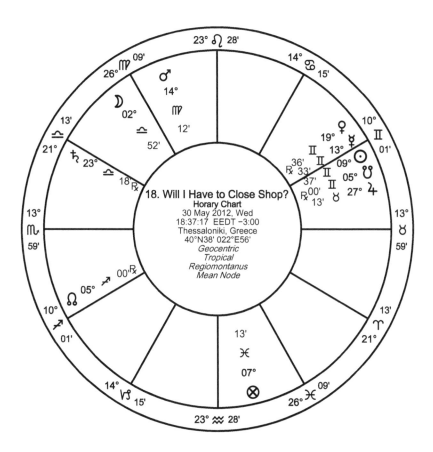

Querent: First house, Mars (1st house domicile ruler and almuten), the Moon.

Shop: Tenth house, the Sun (10th house domicile ruler and almuten and natural significator of professional matters).

Querent's money: Second house, Jupiter (2nd house domicile ruler and almuten, natural significator of wealth and domicile ruler of the Lot of Fortune), the Lot of Fortune, Venus (almuten of the Lot of Fortune), the North Node.

Testimonies for: The Moon is applying to a trine with the Sun. The Moon is in her own face. Mars is in a fortunate house (11th). Jupiter is angular. Mercury receives the Sun and Venus in his domicile (Mercury is also in the terms of Venus, so the reception is mutual). The North Node is conjunct the 2nd house cusp. Mars has a mutual reception with Venus and a (weak) mutual reception with Mercury. The Lot of Fortune is in the fertile sign of Pisces. Venus has a mutual reception with Saturn.

Testimonies against: The Sun is conjunct the South Node and is in the 8th house. He is received by Mercury, but Mercury is combust (though moving away fast). The Sun applies to square Mars without reception (though when the aspect becomes exact, the Sun is going to be in Mars' terms and face). Jupiter is conjunct Algol. The Moon and the Sun don't aspect the ascendant.

Judgement: The situation doesn't look very good. Mercury would have been a great help for both Mars (despite the square) and the Sun, but he is combust and cannot act effectively (he is in domicile though and moving away from combustion and so, he is not destroyed). The Sun in the 8th house, the house of death, is not a positive testimony either. The Sun will square Mars (with reception though, when the aspect perfects). Venus, who intervenes (besides Mercury), is weak by being retrograde, in the 8th house and about to move into combustion (but has mutual receptions with Mercury and Mars). The Sun also weakens by his conjunction with the South Node. However, the North Node conjunction with the 2nd house cusp, the fact that Mercury, although combust, is in his domicile and receives the Sun and Mars and finally, the beneficial trine between the Lights (always a fortunate indication in every chart but especially in work-related charts because the Sun is the natural significator of many 10th house matters and here he is also the 10th house ruler) indicate that all is not quite lost yet. Finally, the presence of the significators in common signs is indicative of change.

Outcome: The querent had to move to a different area in order to save her business (common signs). Although the situation is still touch and go and the danger of closing down is always looming on the horizon and can easily happen at any time, she is still in business five years after the question.

Astrological conclusions: This chart shows that a single reception by domicile or exaltation with conjunction is very strong and helps the received planets a lot. It seems that a combust planet in domicile (possibly also exaltation) is not completely destroyed. Also, being combust but moving away from the Sun is much better than being combust and applying to the Sun.

"When Will I Find a New Job?"

The querent had just lost his job and was wondering when he was going to find a new one.

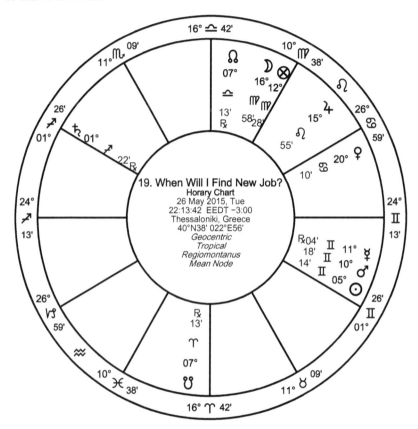

Querent: First house, Jupiter (1st house domicile ruler and almuten), the Moon.

New job: Tenth house, Venus (10th house domicile ruler and co-almuten), Saturn (10th house co-almuten), the Sun (natural significator of professional matters).

Testimonies for: The North Node is conjunct the 10th house cusp. Jupiter trines the ascendant and is in mutual reception with Saturn. The Moon is conjunct the Lot of Fortune. Jupiter is in his own triplicity and face. The Moon is in her own triplicity and applies to a sextile with

Venus (the job) and they have a strong mutual reception. The Fortunes are significators.

Testimonies against: The Sun is in the 6th house, conjunct Mars, an Infortune, and they both oppose Saturn (separating, though). Saturn is retrograde. The Moon is cadent (although in the 10th sign from the ascendant) and afflicted by both the Sun and Mars (but the aspects are separating). Venus is in the 8th house and doesn't aspect the ascendant.

Judgement: This is not the best of charts with both significators of the job in a less than perfect condition (particularly Saturn). However, Saturn, despite the oppositions from the Sun and Mars, is in the same sign as the ascendant (but not afflicting it much) and is helped by the mutual reception with Jupiter. Venus may be in the 8th house, but the Moon applies to her with a sextile and they have a strong mutual reception. It is this aspect, along with the fortunate conjunction of the North Node in the 10th house, that tips the scales into the querent's favour and so he will find a job in a little more than three time units. With Venus in the 8th house, the Moon in a common sign and cadent, months seem more likely than weeks. Given the negative testimonies, the job may not be exactly the job of the querent's dreams.

Outcome: Three months later (25 August), the querent agreed to sign a contract for a new job. The contract was signed on the 9th of September. The pay wasn't particularly good, but, according to the querent, "the job had prospects".

Astrological conclusions: A sextile with reception is usually enough to give us a positive outcome. Once again, the fact that the Moon "hates" Venus by being in the sign of her fall, is of little importance and completely overridden by the real reception.

"Will I Get the Job?"

The querent was told by a third party that there could be a job for him as a columnist in a newspaper. Time was passing by, however, without further news.

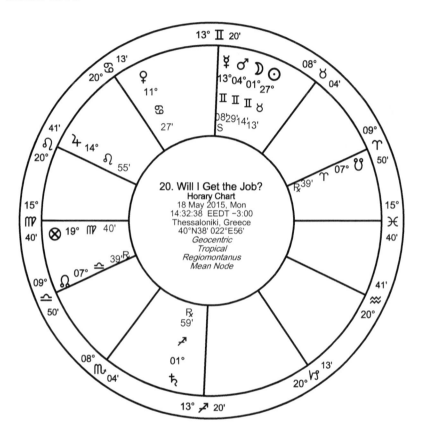

Querent: First house, Mercury (1st house domicile ruler and almuten), the Moon.

Job: Tenth house, Mercury (10th house domicile ruler and almuten). Also, Mars, the Moon, the Sun (natural significator of professional matters).

Testimonies for: Mercury is in domicile and conjunct the Midheaven. The Lot of Fortune is in the 1st house. The Moon is in the same sign as the Midheaven. Mercury receives Mars and the Moon in his own sign.

Testimonies against: Mercury is practically stationary and about to turn retrograde. The Moon will first oppose Saturn and then conjunct Mars, the other Infortune. Mars afflicts the 10th house cusp. The Sun is conjunct Algol.

Judgement: A most unfortunate chart. The sextile of Mercury to Jupiter, a Fortune, will never perfect, as Mercury is about to turn retrograde (refranation). Mercury, by turning retrograde, will conjunct Mars, an Infortune. Most importantly, the Moon applies to both the Infortunes and therefore, the querent will most definitely NOT get the job.

Outcome: Not only didn't he get the job, but there was no job in the end. The newspaper was never launched due to the capital controls.

Astrological conclusions: This chart shows the concept of refranation clearly with Mercury turning retrograde before he perfects the sextile with Jupiter. Once again, the Moon applying to the Infortunes with hard aspects without a strong reception is a very negative testimony.

"Will I Get a Job in Nine Months?"

The querent had gone to another astrologer who told her to set a time frame for the question. I told her I disagree with this sort of question, because what if you find a job in ten months for example? This chart must say no. Anyway, she wanted a second opinion.

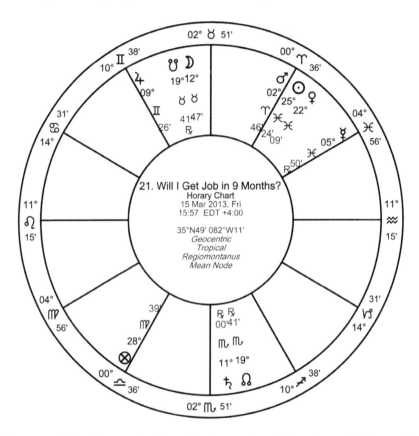

Querent: First house, the Sun (1st house domicile ruler and almuten), the Moon.

New job: Tenth house, Venus (10th house domicile ruler and almuten), the Moon, the South Node, the Sun (natural significator in professional matters).

Testimonies for: The Moon is exalted and angular in the 10th house. Venus is in the sign of her exaltation and she is also in her own triplicity.

The Moon applies to a sextile with Venus with strong reception and the aspect is within orb. The Sun has a mutual reception with Mars, is received by Venus and he is moving to the sign of his exaltation.

Testimonies against: The South Node is in the 10th house. The Moon is afflicted by her recent opposition with Saturn. Venus is combust and in the 8th house.

Judgement: Venus is combust (although she is the Sun's dispositor by exaltation and triplicity and this probably saves her from destruction), but the Sun will change sign first and she will escape combustion for a while (although she would still be under the beams). The Moon's next aspect is a fortunate sextile with a strong reception with Venus, a Fortune, and they are both exalted. However, the South Node is in the 10th house and the Moon's affliction by Saturn is serious (she is separating, though). Still, the very fortunate sextile of the Moon to the 10th house ruler Venus, with the Moon being in the 10th house will almost certainly get the querent a job in approximately 11 time units. It may not be a very good one, though, and there may be problems (Venus will re-enter combustion in Aries).

Outcome: She did indeed find a job in 11 months. However, it didn't last for very long, she had problems with her boss and in the autumn of 2014, she was let go.

Astrological conclusions: It seems that combustion is not destructive when there is a strong reception, no matter who is doing the receiving, although I feel more confident when the Sun is the receiving planet. The South Node in the house of the quesited is a negative testimony.

"Will My Husband Keep His Job for at Least This Year?"
The querent's husband was afraid he might lose his job and his wife asked the question. Every June, the company the husband was working for, decided on such matters. It's the same querent from the previous example and again she had first consulted a different astrologer. She also wanted me to have a look at this chart for a second opinion.

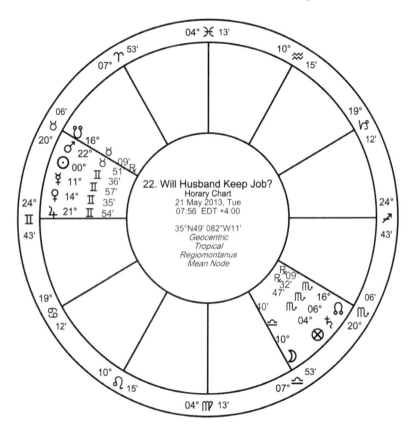

Querent: First house, Mercury (1st house domicile ruler and co-almuten), Saturn (1st house co-almuten), Venus, Jupiter, the Sun, the Moon.

Job: Tenth house, Jupiter (10th house domicile ruler), Venus (10th house almuten), the Sun.

Husband: Seventh house, Jupiter (7th house domicile ruler and almuten).

Testimonies for: The Moon is in the fortunate 5th house. Mercury is direct, very fast and has left combustion. The Sun, Venus and Jupiter are received by Mercury in his domicile. The Moon applies to trine Mercury and Venus with reception and he will eventually trine Jupiter. The Sun, Mercury and the two Fortunes are in the ascending sign.

Testimonies against: Jupiter (the husband) is in detriment and about to go under the beams. The Lot of Fortune is conjunct Saturn. Saturn, co-almuten of the ascendant, is retrograde and doesn't aspect the ascendant. Mercury is under the beams. Common signs prevail, which is indicative of change.

Judgement: A very fortunate chart. All those Gemini planets are received by Mercury and the Moon trines all of them. Mercury may be under the beams, but he is in his domicile and therefore receives the Sun. Venus (almuten of the job) and Mercury apply to conjunct Jupiter (the husband), which can only be a good thing. The husband will most definitely keep his job. However, Jupiter's condition gradually worsens and he will first get under the beams and eventually become combust.

Outcome: The husband did not lose his job in June 2013. The following year however, in June 2014, he was let go.

Astrological conclusions: Once again, combustion or being under the beams is not so destructive when there is reception.

"Will My Husband Find a Job? When?"

The querent's husband (see previous chart) had lost his job. Another question first asked to another astrologer.

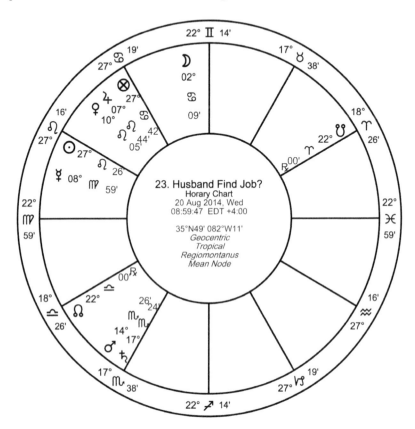

Querent: First house, Mercury (1st house domicile ruler and almuten), the Moon.

Husband: Seventh house, Jupiter (7th house domicile ruler), Venus (7th house almuten).

New job: Tenth house, Mercury (10th house domicile ruler and almuten), the Sun.

Testimonies for: The Moon is in her domicile and so is Mercury. The Moon applies to Mercury with a sextile. The Sun is in his domicile. The

Lot of Fortune is in the fortunate 11th house and the Moon in domicile rules it. Mercury is in the ascending sign. Jupiter is at a safe distance from the Sun and they are moving further apart. Jupiter is conjunct Venus, the other Fortune. Venus and Jupiter are received by the Sun in his domicile.

Testimonies against: Venus moves under the beams and applies to both the Infortunes with a square. Jupiter is also afflicted by the Infortunes (Mars can be considered a benefic here, but we still have a square without a strong reception). The sextile between the Moon and Mercury is without reception. The Sun is in the 12th house.

Judgement: The sextile of the Moon with Mercury looks very promising. A sextile usually needs a reception to be particularly effective, but in this case both Mercury and the Moon are very strong essentially and accidentally. However, this lack of reception together with the affliction of Venus and Jupiter by the Infortunes, raises some doubts (thankfully Venus is received by the Sun). The husband will find a job in 8 units of time (as many degrees as the Moon needs to travel to perfect the aspect with Mercury), but there may be problems.

Outcome: He found a job eight months later and signed the contract on the 15th of April 2015. However, the financial crisis in Greece worsened and he lost his job at the end of May that same year when the possibility of Grexit caused general panic.

Astrological conclusions: The sextile needs a reception to be particularly effective, unless both planets are strongly dignified. Once again, the almuten (Venus) proved its effectiveness. It is the applying aspects of Venus with the Infortunes which show that this will not end well for the husband.

"What's going to happen to me job-wise?"

The querent was unhappy at work and was feeling trapped. However, quitting his job amidst the severe financial crisis in Greece was unthinkable. There was no way out it seemed.

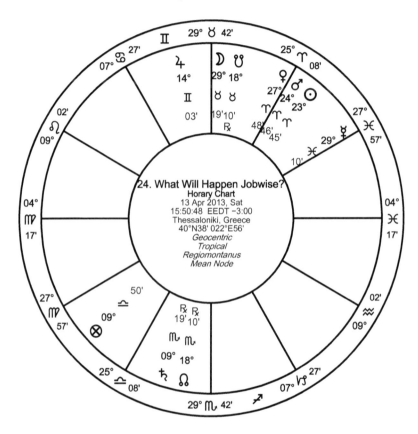

Querent: First house, Mercury (1st house domicile ruler and almuten), the Moon.

Job: Tenth house, Venus (10th house domicile ruler and almuten), the Moon, Mercury (ruler of the intercepted sign in the 10th house), Jupiter, the Sun.

Judgement: Radicality is established by the Moon's conjunction with the 10th house cusp, the house of the quesited. The Moon is not void in course, not only because she is in Taurus at the very end of the sign, but she also makes a partill sextile with Mercury. What is impressive in this chart is that it shows immediate change. The Moon and the MC are about to change sign and so is Mercury, ruler of both the querent and his job. Venus, domicile ruler and almuten of the MC degree, is also in late degrees of Aries. The Sun is exalted and has a mutual reception with Mars, which is a good thing, although they don't aspect the ascendant. The Moon and the MC leaving the fixed sign of Taurus can be explained by the fact that the querent is a civil servant and if he decides to leave, he will abandon the security of public administration (permanent job) and a steady income.

The Lot of Dismissal or Resignation (distance between the Sun and Jupiter and cast from Saturn) is in Sagittarius at 29°33' with Jupiter as his ruler. Jupiter is the next aspect of the Moon. It seems that in less than one time unit, there is going to be a change, which will perhaps lead to the querent's resignation (the post is permanent and so there can be no dismissal). The mutual reception between Mercury and Jupiter (querent and resignation) also points to that direction.

The Moon will conjunct Jupiter in 15 time units and Venus will oppose Saturn in almost 12 time units.

Outcome: Eight months later the querent got sick and was diagnosed with a (not serious) chronic illness. This aggravated his work problems and he simply wanted out. He resigned exactly a year later after the question.

Astrological conclusions: Significators at the end of a sign often indicate change.

"Will I keep my job?"

The querent was working for a firm where they were going to fire some people as a result of the financial crisis. She feared she would be one of those people.

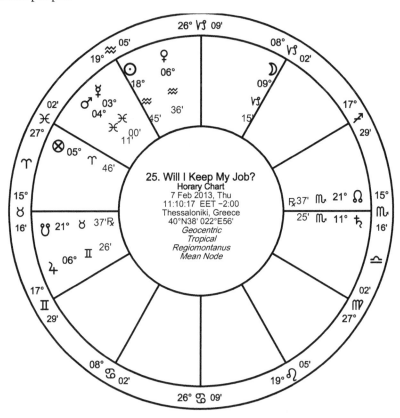

Querent: First house, Venus (1st house domicile ruler and almuten), the Moon, the South Node.

Job: Tenth house, Saturn (10th house domicile ruler), Mars (10th house almuten), the Sun.

Testimonies for: Venus is in the 10th sign from the ascendant (the 10th and the 11th houses are both strong so it doesn't matter where you want to place her), in her own face and makes a partill trine with the other Fortune, Jupiter, who is in his own terms and face. Venus has a mutual reception with Saturn. Mars applies to trine Saturn with mutual reception. The Moon applies to a sextile with Saturn who receives her in his domicile. The Sun is in the fortunate 11th house and has a mutual reception with Saturn. Mercury, the querent's money, though in detriment and conjunct Mars, is in mutual reception with Jupiter, who has more affinity with the 2nd house than the 1st. The ascendant, Venus and Saturn are all in fixed signs, indicating no change.

Testimonies against: Venus is under the beams. Her aspect with Saturn is a square (the mutual reception helps a lot, though). The Moon is in detriment, cadent and has very little light. The South Node is in the ascendant. Mars applies to a square with Jupiter (although Jupiter is a Fortune and he receives Mars). The Sun is in detriment and the aspect with Saturn is a square.

Judgement: The South Node in the 1st house weakens the querent, the Moon is not strong and Venus will square Saturn. The Sun in detriment also squares Saturn, but again there is reception. However, Venus has a mutual reception with Saturn and the Moon applies to sextile Saturn with reception. These are fortunate testimonies which counterbalance the negative testimonies. I reassured the querent that she was not going to lose her job. It's not going to be easy though.

Outcome: She didn't lose her job and she still works there. It has been difficult though.

Astrological conclusions: Difficult aspects and lack of dignity are helped considerably by reception. Once again, if you place too much emphasis on the fact that Saturn "hates" the Moon, you will give the wrong answer.

"Will I do well in the exams?"

The querent decided to sit for an exam a year earlier than when he was supposed to, because he didn't want to spend another year studying. He believed he stood a chance, but, naturally, he was afraid he might not do well.

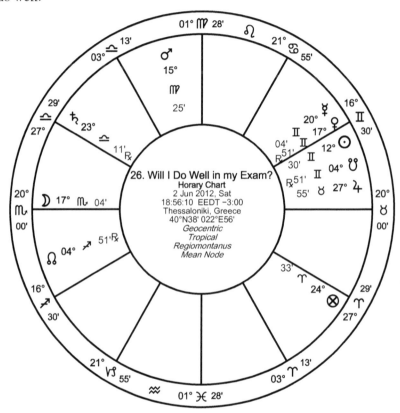

Querent: First house, Mars (1st house domicile ruler and almuten), the Moon.

Success: Tenth house, Mercury (10th house domicile ruler and almuten), Mars.

Testimonies for: Mercury is in domicile, direct, very fast and leaving combustion. The Moon is conjunct the ascendant and Mars receives her. Mars, domicile ruler of the ascendant, is in the 10th house of success. The MC is conjunct Regulus (in Virgo since 2010), a most important and positive testimony in such charts. Venus, who is received by Mercury in his domicile, translates light from Mercury (success) to Mars (querent). Venus and Mars have a mutual reception. Mercury and Mars have a mutual reception. Venus makes a trine to Saturn in exaltation with mutual reception. The Lot of Fortune is ruled by angular Mars in the house of the quesited. The Moon next applies to angular Jupiter and she receives him. Mercury next applies to Saturn in exaltation and Saturn receives him.

Testimonies against: Mars is an Infortune (although with so many receptions, a lot of his malice has gone away). Mercury and Venus are in the 8th house and the South Node is there. The Moon is in fall. Venus is combust (but Venus receives the Sun in her own terms) and it is doubtful whether she can effectively translate light. The aspect between the Moon and Jupiter is an opposition. The Sun applies to square Mars (but Mars disposes the Sun by face).

Judgement: I think it is safe to say that the querent will most certainly pass the exam. The positive testimonies are enough to guarantee that. Will he do well? The Moon conjunct the ascendant is positive, but she is in her fall. Venus, being combust, can't be relied upon to translate light effectively. On the other hand, Regulus conjunct the MC is a very strong testimony and can override some of the negativity in such charts.

Outcome: The written exam was difficult for him, as was expected, but he performed adequately. It was the oral exam that went magnificently and boosted his overall grade.

Astrological conclusions: Reception by domicile with conjunction is very strong. Regulus plays an important role in competition charts and can override some negative testimony.

"Who will win the elections?"

This is one of my own questions and it refers to the elections on the 20th of September 2015. The polls before the elections showed a very close race between the ruling party and the biggest party of the opposition.

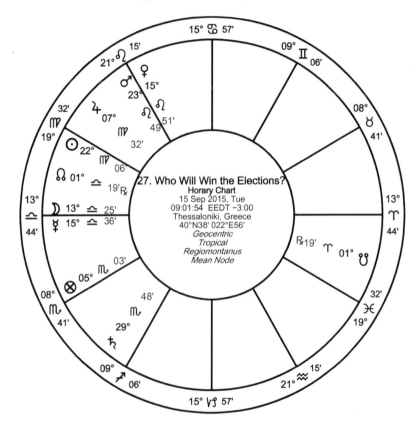

Querent, the people: First house, Venus (1st house domicile ruler), Saturn (1st house almuten), the Moon, Mercury.

Ruling party: Tenth house, the Moon (10th house domicile ruler and almuten).

Opposition: Fourth house, Saturn (4th house domicile ruler and co-almuten), Mars (4th house co-almuten), Venus (4th house co-almuten).

Testimonies in favour of the ruling party: The Moon makes a partill conjunction with the ascendant and applies to a conjunction with Mercury (the people) with reception (at the moment of asking but not when the aspect perfects) and to a sextile with Venus with a strong reception.

Testimonies against the ruling party: The Moon is peregrine (but applies to planets who receive her).

Testimonies in favour of the opposition: Saturn is in his own terms and direct. He also has a mutual reception with Venus (terms/triplicity). Venus is in the fortunate 11th house.

Testimonies against the opposition: Mars squares Saturn (Mars receives Saturn, but we have the two Infortunes here, so we would need a strong mutual reception). Venus is afflicted by Mars and she is very slow. Saturn is about to change sign and by entering Sagittarius, he will lose dignity. Mercury (the people) is even slower than Venus and he will turn retrograde, therefore never perfecting the sextile with her. Finally, Saturn doesn't aspect the ascendant.

Judgement: This chart strongly favours the ruling party. The partill conjunction of the Moon (ruling party) with the ascendant (people) is enough of a testimony to ensure victory in the upcoming elections. The applying conjunction with Mercury also says the same thing and the sextile of the Moon to Venus strengthens them even more. Saturn is not in a bad condition (he is direct and in his terms) and Venus is in the fortunate 11th house but cannot possibly match the testimonies in favour of the ruling party. In fact, the chart promises an easy victory for them and the result is by no means a close race, in spite of what the polls say.

Outcome: It was an easy and clear victory for the government party. The opposition didn't do badly, but were well behind.

Astrological conclusions: Angularity is a very important accidental dignity. Not aspecting the ascendant is a debility.

"Will Greece win the Eurovision song contest?"

It was rumoured that our song would do well, because it was out of the ordinary.

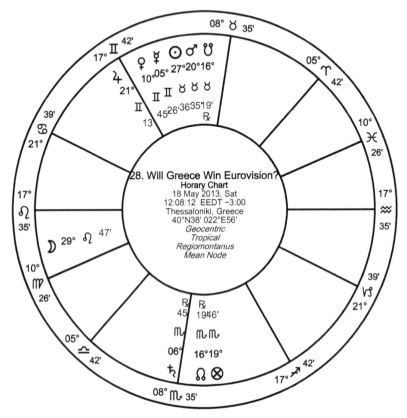

28. Will Greece Win Eurovision?
Horary Chart
18 May 2013, Sat
12:08:12 EEDT −3:00
Thessaloniki, Greece
40°N38′ 022°E56′
Geocentric
Tropical
Regiomontanus
Mean Node

Greece: First house, the Sun (1st house domicile ruler and almuten), the Moon.

Win: Tenth house, Venus (10th house domicile ruler and almuten), Mars, the Sun, the South Node.

The Moon is at the very end of her void course and she has a mutual reception with the Sun, who is at 27° Taurus and was the Moon's previous aspect. It is doubtful, therefore, that she was ever truly void in course.

Testimonies for: The Sun is in the 10th house. The Moon is in the 1st house (the Moon is also the exaltation and face ruler of the MC).

The Sun and the Moon have a strong mutual reception. Venus is in the fortunate 11th house where she is received by Mercury in domicile, free from combustion. Venus applies to the other Fortune, Jupiter (Jupiter is in detriment, though, and there will be no reception when the aspect becomes exact).

Testimonies against: Combust Mars in detriment and the South Node afflict the 10th house by their presence. Saturn, the other Infortune, opposes the MC. The Infortunes are angular. The Sun is afflicted by Mars and he is conjunct Algol.

Judgement: It becomes clear that Greece cannot win with such affliction to the MC. For a win, we would want a chart with no or very few and weak negative testimonies, but that is not the case here. However, the Moon/Sun mutual reception and the good condition of Venus allow us to hope for a good placement.

Outcome: Greece didn't win, but the song came 6th among 26 candidates.

Astrological conclusions: The South Node in the house enquired about is a serious affliction, much like that of the Infortunes whether by presence or hard aspect.

"Will she get the job?"

A client of mine had just lost her job and had applied for a new one. She didn't ask for a horary chart, but opted for a natal chart analysis for the whole year ahead, so I am the querent in this case.

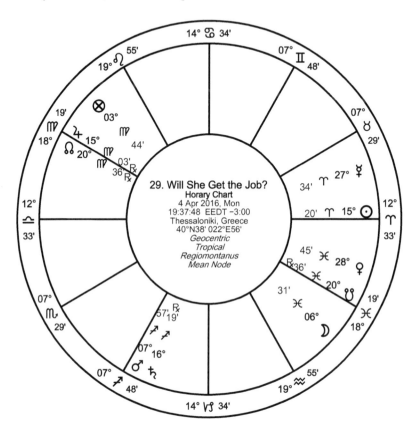

Client: Seventh house, Mars (7th house domicile ruler), the Sun (7th house almuten and also present there), Mercury.

Job: Tenth house, the Moon (10th house domicile ruler and almuten).

Testimonies for: The Moon is received by Venus in the sign of exaltation and her terms. The Sun is angular, in the sign of his exaltation and has a mutual reception with Mars. Mercury has left combustion and he is received by the Sun.

Testimonies against: There is no aspect between the Moon (job) and the Sun or Mercury (both significators of the client). The Moon doesn't aspect the ascendant and she is afflicted by both the Infortunes (she receives Saturn by face, which is somewhat good for Saturn perhaps, but not for her, and, after all, such a weak reception is not enough to counterbalance the square) and she first applies to Mars with a square without reception.

Judgement: It doesn't matter whether one believes I should drop out of the question and give the client the 1st house or give her the 7th house like I did here. The applying squares of the Moon to the Infortunes without a strong reception leave little doubt about the outcome. She won't get the job.

Outcome: She didn't get the job.

Astrological conclusions: Pay attention to this chart. If I had used Ptolemy's table of dignities with Mars as the ruler of the water triplicity by day, then the job (the Moon) would be in the triplicity of Mars which would have been a positive indication, particularly if I stopped seeing Mars as an Infortune because he is a significator here, or if I viewed this as "the job likes the client" thing. Also, the Moon is always a significator in EVERY chart and she is simply NOT only the co-significator of the querent. Once again, therefore, the Moon applying to the Infortunes with a weak or no reception is a very negative testimony, no matter what the question is or who is asking it.

"Will my firm shut down and will I receive severance pay?"
The querent was very unhappy at work, but she didn't want to quit because she would get no severance pay. She was hoping the firm would shut down (it was rumoured that it would do so very soon) and by being laid off, she would receive a handsome sum of money.

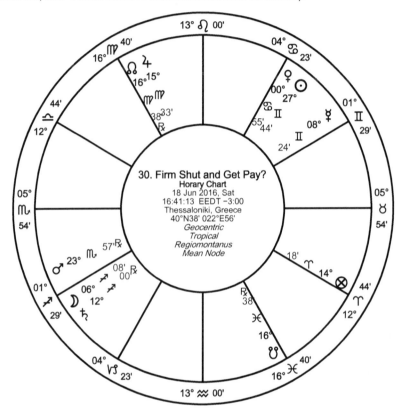

30. Firm Shut and Get Pay?
Horary Chart
18 Jun 2016, Sat
16:41:13 EEDT −3:00
Thessaloniki, Greece
40°N38' 022°E56'
Geocentric
Tropical
Regiomontanus
Mean Node

Querent: First house, Mars (1st house domicile ruler and almuten), the Moon.

Job: Tenth house, the Sun (10th domicile ruler and almuten).

Money: Second house, Jupiter (2nd house domicile ruler and almuten), the Lot of Fortune, Mars (domicile ruler of the Lot of Fortune) and the Sun (almuten of the Lot of Fortune), the Moon, Saturn.

Testimonies for: Mars is in domicile and will soon turn direct. Jupiter has recently turned direct, he is conjunct the North Node and in the fortunate 11th house, where he rejoices. The Sun is received by Mercury, free from the beams and direct, in his domicile. There is a mutual reception between Jupiter and Venus, between Mars and Venus and between the Sun and Saturn.

Testimonies against: Saturn is retrograde and afflicting the house of the quesited. Jupiter is in the sign of his detriment and afflicted by Saturn. The Sun is in the malefic 8th house. The Moon is applying to oppose Mercury, to conjunct Saturn (with a negligible reception), to square Jupiter (with reception) and to oppose the Sun (this is out of orb), all negative aspects. The Lot of Fortune is in the malefic 6th house.

Judgement: The Moon in the 2nd house establishes radicality for the question. The Sun may be in the 8th house, but he is received by Mercury there. So, yes, there are problems at work, but not that serious. The Sun is about to change sign, where he will lose Mercury's help, but he will aspect the ascendant and will not be afflicted by the Infortunes. There doesn't seem to be any serious threat to the company. Retrograde Saturn in the 2nd house is a very negative testimony by itself, but especially here where he squares Jupiter (the querent's money) and also afflicts the Moon. So, no, she won't get the money she hopes for, because, most probably, the company won't shut down. However, the fact that Mars will soon turn direct in Scorpio is a good sign for her.

Outcome: The company didn't shut down and, subsequently, she didn't get any severance pay. Several employees were laid off, but she wasn't one of them. She was transferred to another department, where she is supposedly safe and will work in a better environment, but with a small reduction to her salary. This happened on the 9th of September, a little less than three months later. The Sun needs a little more than two degrees to enter Cancer (change in her job), but he is slow for his standards (0°57') and this took a little longer.

Astrological conclusions: Once again, a conjunction of the Moon with an Infortune with no reception or a weak one gives us the answer. A Saturn without dignity afflicting the house of the quesited is a very negative testimony.

Part Six
Example Charts
Tenth House Matters – Sport

"Will Federer win Australian Open 2013?"

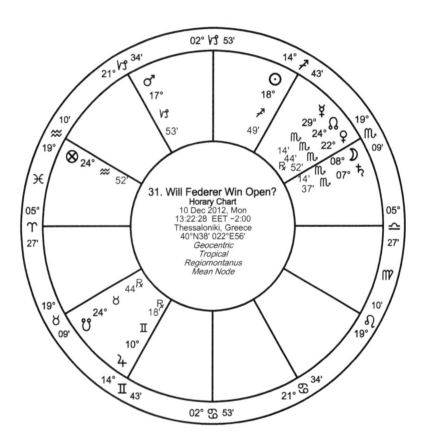

31. Will Federer Win Open?
Horary Chart
10 Dec 2012, Mon
13:22:28 EET −2:00
Thessaloniki, Greece
40°N38' 022°E56'
Geocentric
Tropical
Regiomontanus
Mean Node

Federer: I'm a Federer fan so he gets the first house, Mars (1st house domicile ruler), the Sun (1st house almuten), the Moon.

Win: Tenth house, Saturn (10th house domicile ruler and almuten).

Testimonies for: Mars is exalted and in the 10th house (he is closer to the 11th house, but I consider him to be in the 10th, because Capricorn is the natural tenth sign with an Aries ascendant). Mars and Saturn have a very strong mutual reception by domicile. The Moon translates light from Saturn (win) to Mars (Federer) with a sextile and Mars receives the Moon in his domicile. The Sun is in his triplicity. Mars has a strong mutual reception with Venus. Saturn is received by Venus in her triplicity and terms.

Testimonies against: The Moon is in fall, in the Via Combusta and in the 8th house. Saturn is in the 8th house. The Infortunes are significators. The Moon has very little light and is severely afflicted by Saturn. Venus, who receives Saturn, is in the 8th house and in detriment. Since there is also a big money prize for the winner, the fact that the South Node is in the 2nd house of Federer may also be relevant. The Sun is cadent and doesn't aspect Mars or Saturn.

Judgement: This is quite a good chart, but the affliction of the Moon by Saturn is very serious. For a planet to translate light effectively, it needs to be in a good condition and have receptions with the other two planets. Here, the Moon is very weak and there is a good reception only with Mars and not with Saturn. If the Moon and Saturn were in a better house and sign, perhaps something could be done, but not in this case, because for a grand slam win, we need a nearly flawless chart. However, the positive testimonies are enough to indicate that he will do very well.

Outcome: This was my final test for the QHP Diploma and I predicted he would reach the semi–finals or even the final, but he wouldn't win the trophy. He reached the semi–finals where he lost.

Astrological conclusions: We see yet again that the Infortunes don't lose their Infortune status when they are significators. In this chart the Moon, already in fall, is severely afflicted by Saturn and there can be no trophy despite the very fortunate testimonies elsewhere. An effective translation of light needs receptions between the planets involved and a good condition of the planet who is doing the translation.

"Will Federer win against Nadal?"

Federer was playing against his great opponent Nadal, who was often causing him problems.

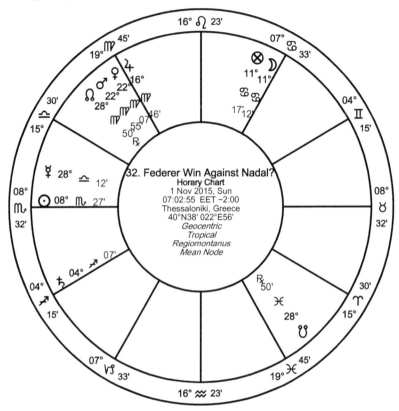

Federer: First house, Mars (1st house domicile ruler and almuten), the Sun, the Moon.

Win: Tenth house, the Sun (10th house domicile ruler and almuten).

Testimonies for: The Sun (win) makes a partill conjunction with the ascendant (Federer). The Moon is in her domicile and trines the ascendant. Mars makes a partill conjunction with Venus, a Fortune, with mutual reception. Mars is in the fortunate 11th house, conjunct the North Node and in his own terms. The Moon is exactly conjunct the Lot of Fortune, which she rules. The Moon will next sextile Jupiter, a Fortune in the house he rejoices, who receives her.

Testimonies against: The Moon is cadent. The Sun is peregrine.

Judgement: An excellent chart. The Sun's conjunction with the ascendant is enough of a testimony to give Federer the win, but the whole chart is very fortunate. There can be no doubt whatsoever that Federer will win the match.

Outcome: Federer won.

Astrological conclusions: The ruler of the quesited in the house of the querent, unless he is an Infortune without dignity or severely afflicted, is a very strong positive testimony. The Moon applying to a Fortune with reception, whether the Fortune is a significator or not, is also very positive.

"Will Federer win against Djokovic?"

Federer was playing against the world No 1 player, Djokovic, who was clearly the favourite. The match had already started and seeing Federer playing very well, I asked the question.

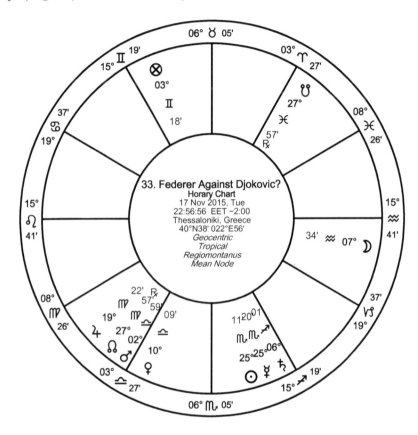

33. Federer Against Djokovic?
Horary Chart
17 Nov 2015, Tue
22:56:56 EET −2:00
Thessaloniki, Greece
40°N38' 022°E56'
Geocentric
Tropical
Regiomontanus
Mean Node

Federer: First house, the Sun (1st house domicile ruler and almuten), the Moon.

Win: Tenth house, Venus (10th house domicile ruler and co–almuten), the Moon (10th house co–almuten).

Testimonies for: Both the Sun (Federer) and the Moon (win, Federer) are angular. Venus (the win) is in her domicile. The Moon applies to Venus with a trine and Venus receives her by terms and face. The Lot of Fortune is ruled by Mercury, who is cazimi (both by longitude and latitude).

Testimonies against: The Sun is peregrine and the Moon applies to square him (it is out of orb, though, and the trine to Venus comes first). Venus is loosely conjunct Mars in detriment (but Venus rules him and has the upper hand).

Judgement: The positive testimonies far outweigh the weak negative ones. Federer should win.

Outcome: He did.

Astrological conclusions: A trine with reception between principal significators is one of the best positive testimonies around.

"Will Federer win against Del Potro?"
Federer was playing against Del Potro, in his hometown, Basel.

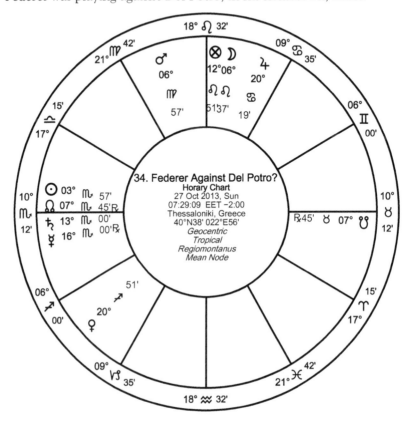

Federer: First house, Mars (1st house domicile ruler and co–almuten), Venus (1st house co–almuten), the Sun, Saturn, Mercury, the Moon.

Win: Tenth house, the Sun (10th house domicile ruler and almuten), the Moon (possibly).

Testimonies for: The 10th house ruler (the Sun) is conjunct the ascendant. Mars is in the fortunate 11th house (he has little affinity with the 10th house) and he has a mutual reception with Mercury. The North Node is in the first house conjunct all the Scorpio planets. The Moon is in the 10th sign from the ascendant and conjunct the Lot of Fortune. Exalted Jupiter trines the ascendant and all the planets there. The Sun applies to sextile with Mars, who receives him in his domicile. Mars and the Sun also have a (weak) mutual reception. Venus and the Sun have a mutual reception by triplicity (no aspect).

Testimonies against: Saturn in the 1st house is a very serious negative testimony, unless he has essential dignity. In this chart, he is under the beams and moving towards combustion. The Moon applies to square Saturn. Mercury is retrograde and under the beams. The Sun/Mars sextile is prohibited by Mercury.

Judgement: There are positive testimonies, but Saturn in the 1st house and the Moon/Saturn square leave little hope for Federer. However, because of the positive testimonies, he won't go away without a fight.

Outcome: Federer did manage to win a set, but in the end he lost 2 sets to 1.

Astrological conclusions: We see again the important role of the Moon in horary charts. If she applies with a hard aspect to an Infortune without reception, there is little hope. Also, an Infortune with no dignity in the house of the querent or quesited is a serious problem. Saturn in the 1st house, according to Lilly, almost always destroys the matter (unless he is dignified).

"Will Greece win the match with Costa Rica in World Cup 2014?"

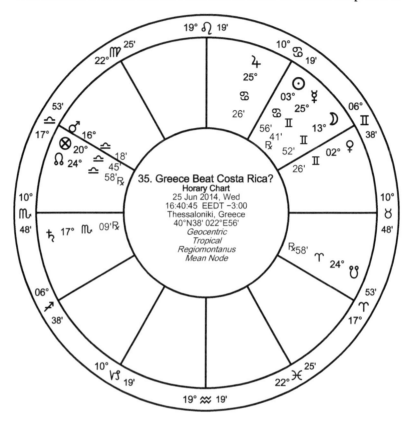

Greece: First house, Mars (1st house domicile ruler and co–almuten), Venus (1st house co–almuten) Saturn, the Moon.

Win: Tenth house, the Sun (10th house domicile ruler and almuten).

Testimonies for: The Sun trines the ascendant and is received by Jupiter in the sign of his exaltation. The Moon applies to a trine with Mars, the ascendant ruler, with a single reception by face. Mars and Saturn are in strong mutual reception (without aspect, though). The Moon is received by Mercury in his domicile. Venus is also received by Mercury in his domicile. The Sun applies to Saturn (out of orb at the moment of asking) with a trine with a weak reception by face. Saturn makes a trine (separating, though) with an exalted Jupiter. There is a mutual reception between Venus and Saturn with no aspect. Venus applies to a trine with Mars with reception (out of orb at the moment of asking).

Testimonies against: The Moon is in the 8th house and Mars is in the 12th house. The mutual reception between Mars and Saturn is not very helpful because there is no aspect and they are both in a poor condition (Mars is in detriment and Saturn is retrograde). The Sun is cadent. Saturn afflicts the 1st house by his presence. Mercury, who receives the Moon and Venus, is retrograde and still under the beams. The Lot of Fortune is in the 12th house afflicted by Mars in detriment.

Judgement: The Moon/Mars trine looks promising, but it takes place in bad houses. The Sun/Saturn trine is not bad, but out of orb and with a weak reception. The mutual reception between Mars and Saturn cannot wipe out Saturn's malice completely because there is no aspect and they are both in poor condition. With Saturn retrograde in the 1st house, Greece can have no real hope for victory. If the Moon/Mars trine had taken place in better houses with a stronger reception and if Saturn had had a strong reception with a fortunate applying aspect, I would have been more hopeful for the Greek team. They will put up a good fight, though, since there are fortunate testimonies.

Outcome: The result was a draw in full and extra time! Greece, however, lost 5–3 on penalties.

Astrological conclusions: Saturn in the 1st house without dignity almost always destroys the matter.

"Will Federer win against Meltzer?"
Federer was playing Meltzer in the 2010 Wimbledon championships.

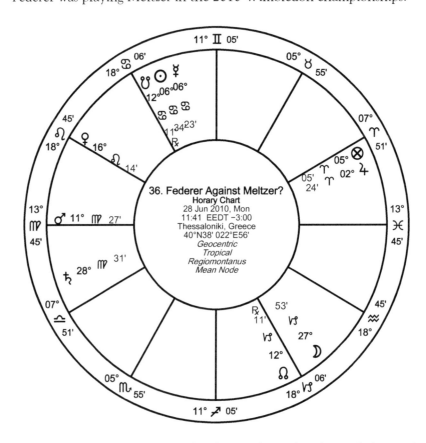

Federer: First house, Mercury (1st house domicile ruler and almuten), Mars, Saturn, the Moon.

Win: Tenth house, Mercury (10th house domicile ruler and almuten).

Testimonies for: Saturn is in his own terms. The Moon applies to a trine with Saturn with a strong reception. The Sun and Mercury apply to a sextile with Mars. Mars receives the Sun in his terms and has a mutual reception (terms/domicile, exaltation) with Mercury. Saturn and Venus have a mutual reception (terms/triplicity). Most importantly, Mercury is cazimi (by longitude only).

Testimonies against: The Sun and Mercury are conjunct the South Node. Mars and Saturn afflict the ascendant. The Moon is in detriment.

Judgement: Mercury conjunct the South Node and both the Infortunes in the ascending sign would normally be enough of a testimony for a negative result, despite the receptions. Can Mercury cazimi (with the help of the other positive testimonies) turn the tables in Federer's favour?

Outcome: Apparently he can. Federer won easily.

Astrological conclusions: Mercury here is not only the ruler of the querent, but also the ruler of the 10th house, so the fact that he is cazimi helps both querent and quesited. It seems that cazimi only by longitude is valid (although this should be tested on a lot more charts as well). Why didn't Saturn destroy the matter, since he is in the 1st house? Because he is direct and in his own terms, which was not the case in the previous examples. This doesn't mean that this is a strong positive testimony, it just means that Saturn's presence isn't destructive, especially considering that the Moon is applying to a trine with him with a strong reception. Mars conjunct the ascendant, another negative testimony, is not destructive here either, because he has a mutual reception with Mercury. Still, without the cazimi, the outcome might have been different; both the Infortunes in the ascendant seems a bit too much. Finally, if I had used Ptolemy's terms, Saturn wouldn't have been in his own terms and that would have been much worse.

"Will Federer win against Cilic?"

The game had started (Wimbledon 2016 quarterfinals). The opponent (Cilic) was playing very well in the first set and Federer was in trouble.

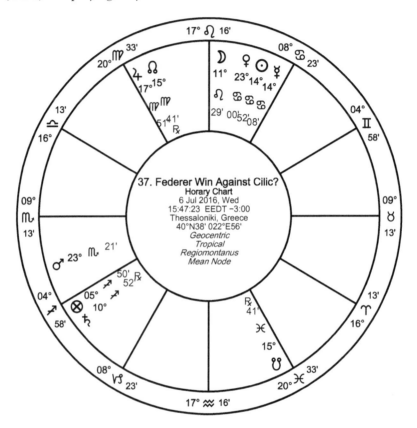

Federer: First house, Mars (1st house domicile ruler and almuten), the Moon.

Win: Tenth house, the Sun (10th house domicile ruler and almuten), the Moon.

Testimonies for: The Moon is in the house of the quesited. Mars is in his domicile, in the 1st house. Mars is in a partill trine with Venus, a Fortune, with reception. The Sun (win) is applying to a sextile with Jupiter, a Fortune, with reception and his next aspect after this one will be a trine with Mars. The Sun and the Moon are in a strong mutual reception (without aspect, though). The Sun is in the house of his joy.

Testimonies against: The Moon is applying to a square with Mars without reception (although when the square actually perfects, the Moon will be in Mars' face). The Sun is cadent. Mars is very slow (he has recently turned direct).

Judgement: The chart is not unfortunate and seems to "disagree" with what was happening on court. The only problem is the square of the Moon to Mars without reception at the moment of asking. However, Mars is not a true malefic here, since he is in his domicile, nocturnally placed and forms harmonious aspects with both of the Fortunes and the Moon is strong by being in the 10th house and helped by the mutual reception with the Sun. Still, a square without reception is always a problem, big or small, but the rest of the testimonies are fortunate and, as a result, Federer must win with difficulty.

Outcome: Federer lost the first set and he went on to lose the second set as well. Just when it seemed impossible for him to turn the match around, he did. He won the third set, he faced matchpoints in the fourth, but managed to win it and finally, he won the fifth set and, therefore, the match.

Astrological conclusions: Dignified Infortunes may not become Fortunes, but they create few, if any, problems. This chart also stresses the importance of the good fortune of the whole chart, besides the significators.

"Will Federer win Wimbledon 2016 semi–finals?"

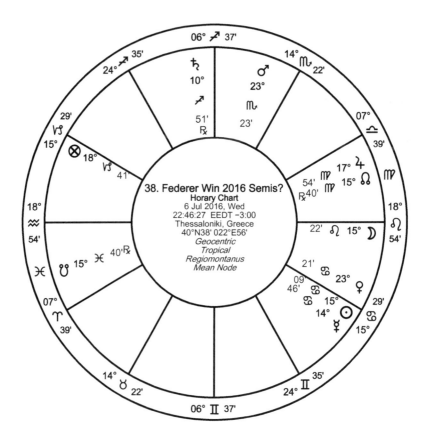

Federer: First house, Saturn (1st house domicile ruler and almuten), Jupiter (domicile ruler of the intercepted sign in the 1st house), the Moon.

Win: Tenth house, Jupiter (10th house domicile ruler and almuten), Saturn.

Testimonies for: Saturn, principal significator of the querent, is in the house of the quesited and, therefore, angular. Jupiter is in his own terms and he is conjunct the North Node. The Sun is applying to a sextile with Jupiter with reception. The Moon is angular (but opposite the ascendant).

Testimonies against: The Moon is applying to a square with Mars without reception (although Mars is essentially dignified and correctly placed in the nocturnal part of a nocturnal chart – see previous chart). Jupiter doesn't aspect the ascendant and is in the sign of his fall. The South Node is in the 1st house. Saturn is an Infortune out of sect, retrograde and afflicts the 10th house by his presence.

Judgement: This is not a fortunate chart. Saturn is an Infortune in bad condition and despite him being the principal significator of Federer and in the 10th house, his presence in the 10th house is not good, as explained in the introduction of this book. Jupiter doesn't aspect the ascendant and the South Node weakens the 1st house. The Moon, finally, doesn't help at all (Mars is a benefic here, but the square with the Moon is without reception). Perhaps the angularity of Saturn, the sextile between the Sun and Jupiter and the fact that Mars is a benefic in this chart can help Federer play a tough match, but I fail to see how he is going to win this.

Outcome: Surprisingly, Federer played very well and was close to winning the match in the fourth set, but a double fault turned the match around. Milos Raonic, his opponent, won the fourth and fifth set, and, therefore, the match.

Astrological conclusions: Once again, the Infortunes don't stop being Infortunes when they are significators. An Infortune without dignity afflicts the house he is in.

Part Seven
Example Charts

First/Sixth/Eighth House Matters – Health, Sickness and Death

"Will my blood test results be OK?"
The querent hadn't had a blood test for a long time and he was worried.

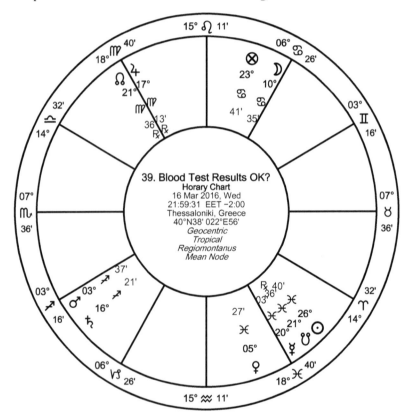

39. Blood Test Results OK?
Horary Chart
16 Mar 2016, Wed
21:59:31 EET −2:00
Thessaloniki, Greece
40°N38' 022°E56'
Geocentric
Tropical
Regiomontanus
Mean Node

Querent: First house, Mars (1st house domicile ruler and almuten), the Moon. Other significators: Jupiter, as the natural significator of blood.

Testimonies for: The Moon is in her domicile and also in hayz. Exalted Venus in her own terms makes a trine with the ascendant. The Moon applies to a sextile with Jupiter with mutual reception. The Lights (vitality) are involved in a grand trine with the ascendant. Jupiter is in his own terms, in conjunction with the North Node and in the house of his joy. Jupiter has a mutual reception with Mercury and with Venus.

Testimonies against: Jupiter (blood) is in detriment and retrograde. Jupiter makes a square with Saturn (with reception though). Mars is very slow and doesn't aspect the ascendant. The Moon is cadent. Jupiter is opposite the Sun (with reception). The Sun is conjunct the South Node.

Judgement: This is quite a fortunate chart. The Moon is especially strong and applies to Jupiter, a Fortune with mutual reception. Mars is slow, but the good thing is that he won't perfect the conjunction with Saturn. Jupiter has essential and accidental dignity, but his T–square with the Sun and Saturn and the fact that he is retrograde and in detriment weakens him. The results are going to be OK, but not perfect.

Outcome: The results generally pleased the querent, because most of the values were normal. Only his cholesterol levels were borderline high and his white cell count was a little high due to rhinitis.

Astrological conclusions: In most medical charts, our main job is to say whether things are going to get better or worse. We are not doctors and most of us are incapable of applying traditional medicine. Our main job as astrologers, therefore, is to say what happens next. If the ruler(s) of the ascendant or of the sick person (if you prefer to turn the chart) and the Moon are not afflicted, or are moving away from affliction, and applying with harmonious aspects to the Fortunes or benefics, then the patient's condition will improve. If not, they are going to get worse. In this case, the Moon is strong and applies to a Fortune and Mars will not perfect the conjunction with Saturn. True, he will eventually turn retrograde, but it's still quite far and we are talking about imminent results here.

"Will I overcome my addiction?"

The querent was battling a drug addiction for which he had recently received help. He was going through a very difficult time and was worried that the addiction would get the better of him.

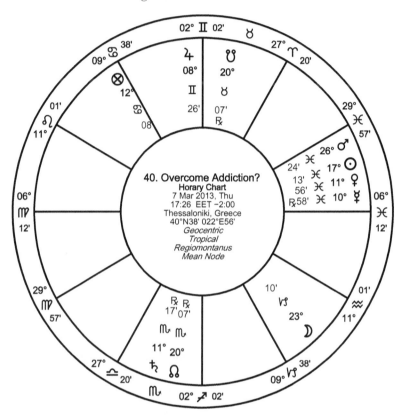

Mercury, the ascendant ruler, is combust and normally I wouldn't judge this chart, but it's a medical question and the combustion is relevant, particularly in this case as the Sun is the ruler of the 12th house of self–undoing.

Querent: First house, Mercury (1st house domicile ruler and almuten), the Moon.

Addiction: Twelfth house (self–undoing), the Sun (12th house domicile ruler and almuten), Saturn (possibly – natural ruler of narcotics according to Al Biruni and, of course, he rejoices in the 12th house).

Testimonies for: Mercury is angular and about to leave combustion. Mercury is in strong mutual reception with Jupiter and is conjunct angular Venus, a Fortune, in the sign of her exaltation, who receives him. The Moon is in her triplicity and applies to a sextile with Mars, who receives her in his exaltation. The Fortunes are angular.

Testimonies against: Mercury will be under the beams after leaving combustion and in the sign of his detriment and fall. Mercury is also retrograde. The Moon is in detriment. The mutual reception between Mercury and Jupiter is not incredibly helpful, since they square each other and are both in detriment.

Judgement: Mercury combust, in detriment and fall and the Moon also in detriment show the dire state the querent is in. However, Mercury leaving combustion and turning direct and the Moon's fortunate applying sextile with Mars indicate that there is going to be an improvement. I told the querent that things will get better and that the addiction will stop having such a hold on him. Still, things are going to be difficult for quite some time. Mercury will be under the beams and in the sign of his detriment and fall for a long time.

Outcome: I talked to the querent five months later and he confirmed that things got a lot better. However, three years after the question, he admitted that the battle was not over yet.

Astrological conclusions: The same conclusion as the previous chart. If the condition of the main significators improves, things get better.

"What will happen with my acne?"
The querent had developed adult acne and was worried.

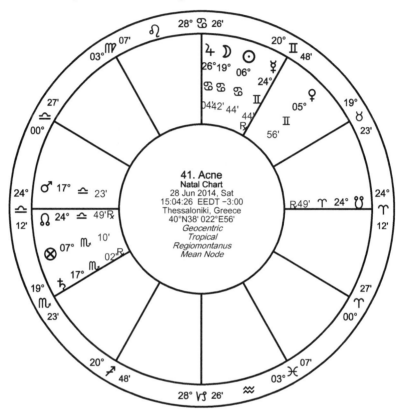

Querent: First house, Venus (1st house domicile ruler and co–almuten), Saturn (1st house co–almuten), Mars, the Moon, the North Node.

Acne: Mars and the Sun, natural significators of pimples on the face. Mars is also the domicile ruler of the 6th house and the Sun is the almuten of the 6th house.

Testimonies for: The Moon is in domicile, very close to the MC. The Moon applies to Jupiter with a very strong mutual reception. Mars has a mutual reception with Saturn. The North Node is conjunct the ascendant. Spica, a very fortunate fixed star, is on the ascendant. Saturn forms trines with the Sun, the Moon and Jupiter. Venus applies to trine Mars and she receives him. Venus is received by Mercury in his domicile.

Testimonies against: Mars is conjunct the ascendant. The Moon is afflicted by Mars. The Moon is under the beams. Mars is in detriment and slow. Venus is cadent or in the 8th house, whichever way you want to see it. Saturn is retrograde and doesn't aspect the ascendant.

Judgement: It is obvious that Mars is responsible for the querent's acne. He is conjunct the ascendant (face), he is the Moon's previous aspect and also rules the sixth house of illness (Aries is also the sign of acne). The Moon is also under the beams of the Sun, confirming that the nature of the disease is hot and dry (acne usually is, that's why it's most common in adolescence, the hot and dry period of life). Mars afflicts the ascendant and the Moon is in Cancer, confirming that the disease is on the face. Mars is in a hot and moist sign and the Sun in a cold and moist sign, either indicating that the fire is not excessive or that the fire is suppressed in the body and erupting through the face. Mars rules the second house of food and Saturn afflicts it by his presence. The querent had recently given up smoking and had put on a lot of weight at the same time his skin was breaking out.

The fact that the Moon is moving away from Mars, is increasing in light and applies to angular Jupiter, a Fortune, with such a strong reception, indicates that his condition will improve. Venus, Mars' dispositor, applying to a trine with him, is also positive. However, Mars has still a long way to go in Libra and the Sun applies to a square with him. The conjunction between the Moon and Jupiter perfects in 6.5 degrees, Mars leaves Libra and enters Scorpio, his domicile, in 12.5 degrees (he is slow though, so this may take longer) and Venus perfects the trine with Mars in 18 degrees approximately.

Outcome: Early the following year the condition started to improve. By summer that same year, the improvement was clearly evident and by the end of the year, the acne was practically gone.

Astrological conclusions: It's not always easy to find the elemental nature of the disease. Is this given by the 6th house and its ruler? Or by the ascendant, its ruler and the Moon and their previous aspects? Should one examine all of these factors? Most probably, yes. In this example, however, Mars is conjunct the ascendant, he is the Moon's previous aspect and is also the 6th house domicile ruler, so he is certainly the culprit.

"Will her father die any moment now?"

I got a call from a friend telling me that her terminally ill father was probably dying in a matter of hours. I decided to cast a chart to confirm this.

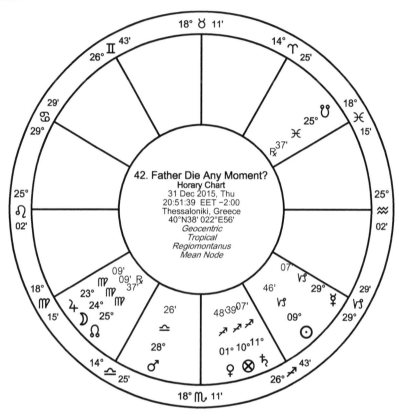

Friend's dad: Second house (fourth house from the eleventh house), Mercury (2nd house domicile ruler and almuten and also ruler of the Lot of the Father at 23°41' Virgo), Jupiter, the Moon. The Lot of the Father is taken from the Sun to Saturn by day and cast from the ascendant. In nocturnal charts, like this one, it is taken from Saturn to the Sun and cast from the ascendant.

Death: Radical eighth house, Jupiter (8th house domicile ruler and almuten), turned eighth house (radical 9th), Mars (9th house domicile ruler and co–almuten), the Sun (9th house co–almuten), Saturn (the other Infortune).

Signification will also be taken from the radical chart, therefore Mars for the father and Mercury for death. If we follow Lilly and other sources, who claim that we should use the ascendant for the sick person, then the Sun would also be a significator of the father.

Testimonies for: Mercury is leaving Capricorn and entering his own terms and triplicity in Aquarius. Mercury and the Moon form a trine with mutual reception. Mercury is separating from Mars, ruler of the turned 8th house in his own terms, and they have a mutual reception. The Moon is in her own triplicity and is conjunct the North Node. Mars, also ruler of the radical fourth house, will leave Libra, the sign of his detriment, and enter Scorpio, the sign of his domicile. The Sun is free from the Infortunes. The Moon is separating from Jupiter, ruler of the radical 8th house.

Testimonies against: Jupiter, ruler of the radical 8th house, is in detriment and inside the 2nd house of the friend's father. The Moon is translating light from Jupiter (death) to Mercury (father). Jupiter, also significator of the friend's father, will turn retrograde soon and will eventually square Saturn, an Infortune.

Judgement: The fact that Mercury has just separated from Mars shows that her father had indeed been unwell, but even if the aspect was applying, death would be unlikely because of the mutual reception. Mercury's condition will improve by entering Aquarius. Mars, another significator of the father, will strengthen by entering Scorpio and the Moon is free from the Infortunes. Most importantly, the translation of light between Jupiter (radical 8th house ruler) and Mercury (one of the father's significators) is not threatening at all because of the trines, the reception between Mercury and Jupiter and the mutual reception between the Moon and Mercury. No, death was not imminent. In the long run, the Jupiter/Saturn square will be a problem, but not now.

Outcome: He survived the crisis and died about three months later.

Astrological conclusions: Mutual reception (or even a strong single reception with a fortunate aspect) between the patient's significator and the significator of death, is a strong positive testimony.

"Will my father get better?"
The querent's father was ill in hospital and the family feared the worst.

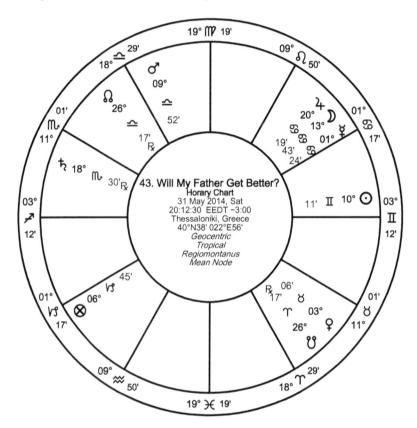

43. Will My Father Get Better?
Horary Chart
31 May 2014, Sat
20:12:30 EEDT −3:00
Thessaloniki, Greece
40°N38' 022°E56'
Geocentric
Tropical
Regiomontanus
Mean Node

Querent's father: Fourth house, Jupiter (4th house domicile ruler), Venus (4th house almuten and ruler of the Lot of the Father at 11°31' Taurus), the Sun (natural significator of fathers in diurnal charts). Jupiter is also the domicile ruler and almuten of the 1st house, if one wants to give the 1st house to the sick person.

Testimonies for: The Moon is in domicile and applies to a conjunction with an exalted Jupiter with a strong mutual reception. The Moon has a mutual reception with Venus, a Fortune. Venus, almuten of the 4th house, is in her domicile, in her triplicity and her own terms. Jupiter is also in his own terms. The Sun is angular and not afflicted.

Testimonies against: The Moon is an accidental malefic by ruling the 8th house, and both the Moon and Jupiter are inside the 8th house. Venus doesn't aspect the ascendant. The Moon is afflicted by her recent square with Mars and first applies to Saturn, the almuten of the turned 8th house (with a trine, though).

Judgement: The Moon, ruler of the 8th house, applies to conjunct Jupiter, ruler of the 4th house of the father (and ruler of the 1st) and this would normally be negative, but in this case, they are both dignified and they have a very strong mutual reception. The Moon is separating from Mars and the trine with Saturn is not going to be a problem, not only because of the nature of aspect, but also because of her essential dignity. Jupiter and Venus, the significators of the father, are very strong essentially. The father is going to get better. However, the applying opposition between Venus and Saturn (out of orb at the moment), which perfects in 14.5 degrees approximately, could cause problems in the future.

Outcome: He got a lot better and left the hospital. In early August 2015, however, he was diagnosed with brain cancer.

Astrological conclusions: Strong essential dignity and mutual reception override accidental debility. The new diagnosis more than a year later was shown by the almuten (also ruler of the Lot of the Father) and not the domicile ruler.

"When will my father die?"

We are talking about the father of the previous example. When he was diagnosed with brain cancer, the querent asked the question. The doctors told her that her father had two months to live, which was the average life expectancy for cases like this, or five months at the most.

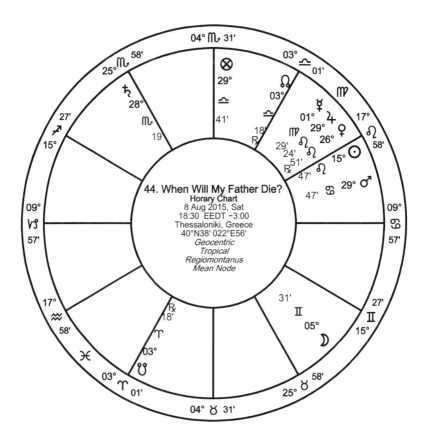

44. When Will My Father Die?
Horary Chart
8 Aug 2015, Sat
18:30 EEDT –3:00
Thessaloniki, Greece
40°N38' 022°E56'
Geocentric
Tropical
Regiomontanus
Mean Node

Querent's father: Fourth house, Venus (4th house domicile ruler and almuten), the Sun (natural significator of fathers in diurnal charts and also co–almuten of the Lot of the Father at 22°29' Aries), Mars (co–almuten of the Lot of the Father).

Testimonies for: The Moon applies to sextile the Sun. The Sun receives Venus in his domicile. Mars will leave Cancer, where he is in fall, and will enter Leo where he will be received by the Sun.

Testimonies against: Venus is retrograde, under the beams and moving towards combustion. The Sun is also the 8th house ruler and applies to a square with Saturn. The sextile between the Moon and the Sun is without reception.

Judgement: The fact that the Sun receives Venus by domicile makes the combustion less dangerous, but in this case the querent's father is terminally ill, so no recovery can be expected. Venus is retrograde and the conjunction with the Sun perfects in almost seven degrees. It's difficult to find the exact timing because the Sun is slow (longer), while the conjunction with Venus is mutually applying (therefore sooner). The conjunction will happen in a succedent house and in a fixed sign, so months seem more probable than weeks. However, taking into account what the doctors said, it must be weeks. If the combustion in this case is in some way protective (or rather, not as destructive) because of the reception, Venus will lose "protection" when the Sun moves into Virgo and the reception with the Sun by domicile is gone. When the Sun moves into Virgo, Venus will have travelled eight and a half degrees or thereabouts, but her retrograde motion indicates a sudden event.

Outcome: No, it wasn't weeks, it was exactly eight months! (Venus losing the protection of the Sun probably). He withered away slowly feeling no pain. The doctors were greatly surprised he lived that long.

Astrological conclusions: When the Sun receives the combust planet, especially by domicile or exaltation, combustion is not completely destructive.

"Am I going to get better?"

The querent was battling a urinary tract infection for months that never seemed to go away completely and she had taken a lot of antibiotics.

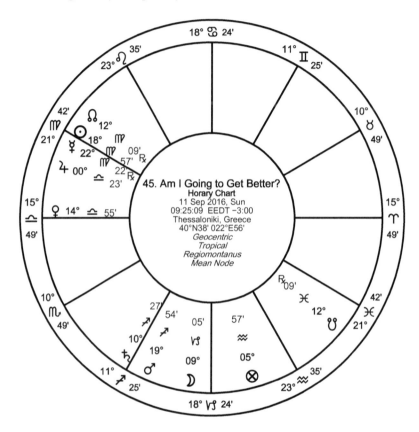

Querent: First house, Venus (1st house domicile ruler), Saturn (1st house almuten), the Moon.

Testimonies for: Venus in domicile is conjunct the ascendant. Saturn has recently been afflicted by Mars and the Sun, but they are both separating from him. Saturn has a very strong mutual reception with Jupiter and they sextile each other. Venus and Jupiter have a mutual reception. Venus forms a sextile with Saturn with reception.

Testimonies against: The Moon is applying to a square with Venus, but since Venus is a Fortune in domicile and receives the Moon in her triplicity, this is more of a fortunate testimony than a negative one. The Moon is in the sign of her detriment.

Judgement: A very fortunate chart. The two Fortunes dignified and unafflicted in the ascending sign is all you need in a question about health. Saturn is protected by the strong mutual reception with Jupiter and the Moon/Venus square is not a problem. She will most definitely get a lot better.

Outcome: I called the querent in early October and she said that she had a urine test twice and everything was fine according to the doctors.

Astrological conclusions: The same conclusion as in previous charts.

"What's next?"

The querent had just found out that her mother had been diagnosed with bone cancer and the doctors told them there was an 80% chance the cancer was aggressive.

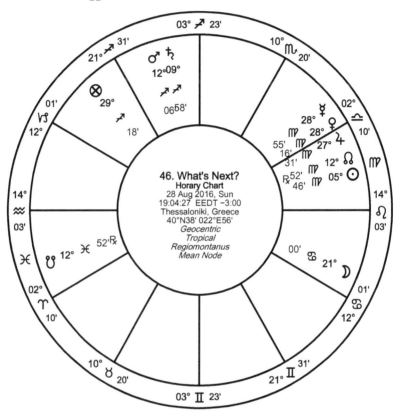

Querent's mother: Tenth house, Jupiter (10th house domicile ruler and almuten and ruler of the Lot of Mothers at 6°48' Sagittarius), Saturn, Mars, Venus (natural significator of mothers in diurnal charts). If one wants to use the 1st house for the mother, like Lilly, then Saturn and Jupiter are the significators again, so there is no contradiction. The Lot of the Mother is taken from Venus to the Moon by day and cast from the ascendant. By night, it is taken from the Moon to Venus and cast from the ascendant.

Testimonies for: The Moon is in her domicile and applies to sextile Jupiter and Venus with reception. Jupiter and Venus are received by

Mercury in his domicile. Venus is in her own triplicity and in a partill conjunction with Mercury in domicile with mutual reception. Mars, although he still afflicts Saturn, is separating from him. Venus and Jupiter are about to enter Libra, where Venus is going to be in her domicile, and Jupiter will be in a wonderful mutual reception with Saturn.

Testimonies against: The Moon is the radical 6th house domicile ruler and applies to aspect two of the mother's significators (she is a benefic here, though, and there is reception). Venus is in the sign of her fall and she is the domicile ruler of the radical 8th house and the turned 6th house. Mercury, the ruler of the turned 8th house, is about to turn retrograde and make an exact conjunction with Venus and Jupiter again. The Sun applies to square Saturn (with reception, though).

Judgement: I'm not worried about the Moon and Mercury being accidental malefics, because they are benefics here and they have strong receptions and make fortunate aspects. Mars separating from Saturn is also a positive indication. The most positive factor however, is the very strong mutual reception between Jupiter and Saturn (almuten of the 8th house), when Jupiter moves into Libra in two and a half units of time. The only thing that worries me is the applying square between the Sun and Saturn, but since there is reception, and combined with the other positive testimonies, I doubt that it means death. Another worrying testimony is the fact that the Sun applies to conjunct Jupiter, but when Jupiter becomes combust, both he and the Sun will be in Libra and Jupiter will have a very strong mutual reception with Saturn.

The vast majority of the significators are in dry signs, either hot or cold. It seems that the mother needs moisture and I suggested a diet of a moist nature. Anyway, we know that she has cancer, but I told the querent that the testimonies look promising and imminent death is not on the cards. In fact, she can expect some sort of improvement, if that's possible. The querent found it very difficult to believe me.

Outcome: Around three weeks after the question, the querent's mother was told that the cancer was not aggressive at all and she belonged to the fortunate 20% of cases like hers. That meant that she would not receive chemotherapy treatment, but would instead be given some pills.

In early January 2017, new test results showed that the tumour had shrunk.

Astrological conclusions: Even if the rulers of the 6th or the 8th house form applying aspects with the patient's significators, there is no harm done if the aspects are harmonious and there are strong receptions. Again, a mutual reception between the significator of the sick person and the significator of death is a very positive testimony.

Part Eight
Example charts
Various Issues

"Should I wait until Mercury turns direct?"
This is not a professional question (I don't accept "should I?" questions), but a question from a friend. I told her what I think about these questions, but she urged me to have a look. The question was about when to sign the contract for the purchase of a flat. According to her, everything was OK with the flat. There was a tenant inside, but the seller told her he would go, once the contract was signed. The only thing that worried her was Mercury retrograde. I told her I would treat the chart as a "Will the deal go through?" one.

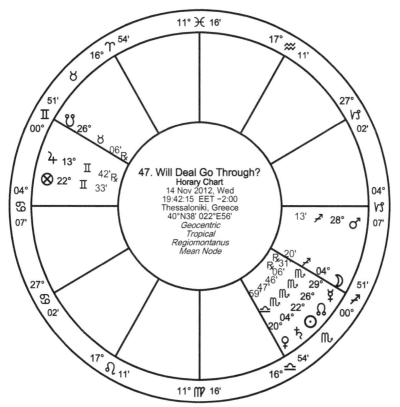

Querent: First house, the Moon (1st house domicile ruler and co–almuten), Mars (1st house co–almuten).

Seller: Seventh house, Saturn (7th house domicile ruler and almuten).

Flat: Fourth house, Mercury (4th house domicile ruler and almuten), the Moon (natural significator of property).

Testimonies for: Mars is in his own terms and in the house of his joy. Saturn has just left the sunbeams. The Lot of Fortune is in the 1st house.

Testimonies against: The Moon is in the cadent and malefic 6th house. The Moon's next aspect is an opposition with Jupiter retrograde and in detriment (with reception, though). Mercury, the flat, is retrograde and combust. Mars is cadent and doesn't aspect the ascendant. There is no aspect between the Moon and Saturn and neither is there one between Mars and Saturn. The Moon and Saturn are peregrine. Finally, there are no aspects between the Moon or Mars (querent) and Mercury (the flat).

Judgement: A most unfortunate chart. There are no aspects between the main significators and the condition of the flat seems awful. I told the querent that her problem was not Mercury retrograde, but that I doubt sincerely that there is ever going to be a deal. She was greatly surprised and had difficulty in believing me, especially the part about the flat, which she described as perfect.

Outcome: It turned out that the tenant had just moved there six months before and the seller wanted a sum of money from the querent before he told the tenant to vacate the flat. The querent refused and there was no deal.

Astrological conclusions: A typical example of misfortune. No aspects between the principal significators and serious debility.

"Will we be able to sell or rent my husband's house?"
The querent's husband bought an old house with a view to renovating
and re–selling it. The renovation works were taking too long a time and
the mortgage payments were a huge burden. This is also a question asked
first to another astrologer.

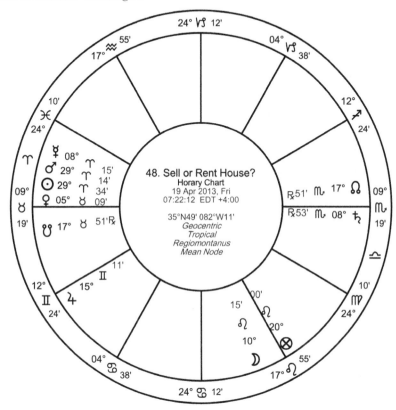

Querent: First house, Venus (1st house domicile ruler and almuten).

Husband: Seventh house, Mars (7th house domicile ruler and almuten),
Saturn.

House: Tenth house (the husband's 4th house), Saturn (10th house
domicile ruler and almuten), the Moon (natural significator of property
and domicile ruler/co–almuten of the radical 4th house), Jupiter (co–
almuten of the radical 4th house).

Signification is also taken from the unturned chart.

Testimonies for: The Moon applies to a sextile with Jupiter with a weak reception. Venus, a Fortune, is in domicile and conjunct the ascendant. Mars in domicile has a strong mutual reception with the Sun in exaltation which helps with the combustion. The North Node is inside the husband's house.

Testimonies against: Mars is about to enter Taurus, the sign of his detriment, where he will be combust without the helpful reception with the Sun. Venus applies to an opposition with Saturn (she receives Saturn though in her triplicity). Saturn is retrograde, and afflicts the 7th house. Jupiter (co–almuten of the radical 4th house) is in detriment, peregrine and doesn't aspect the ascendant. Venus is under the beams and although separating from the Sun, she is about to become combust when the Sun changes sign (although the combustion is not totally destructive as Venus is in her domicile). The Sun, ruler of the Lot of Fortune, is about to enter Taurus and lose dignity. The Moon is afflicted by Saturn. The Sun and Mars are in the 12th house.

Judgement: A very unfortunate chart. The only positive testimony is the Moon/Jupiter sextile (not very fortunate actually, as Jupiter is peregrine, in detriment and the reception is very weak), while all the others are negative. Saturn in the 7th house shows that the house is indeed a burden for the husband. Mars (the husband), by entering Taurus, will be very weak and will oppose Saturn (the house). The oppositions between Venus and Mars with Saturn cannot possibly lead to a successful sale or lease of the property.

Outcome: The house was never sold or rented to anyone. The husband lost his job the next year, he stopped paying the instalments and the bank foreclosed the house.

Astrological conclusions: Significators about to move in the next sign show change, either for better or worse. Oppositions with the Infortunes without a strong mutual reception almost always give negative results. Even a strong mutual reception cannot take away the malice of the aspect completely.

"Where is the USB stick?"

A lot of important files were stored in this USB stick and the querent was anxious to find it.

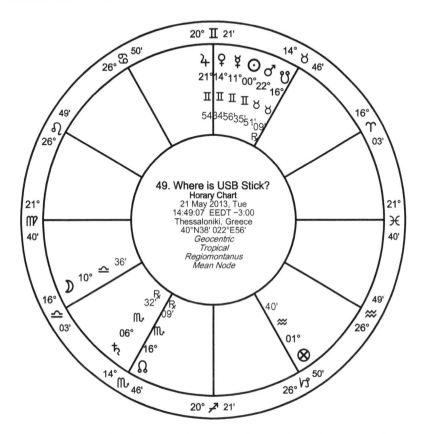

With questions like this one, I limit myself to telling the client whether they will find the lost item or not. It's no use trying to locate an item in places you have no idea about. Half of the time (or more) you are going to be wrong or not specific enough to help the client.

Querent: First house, Mercury (1st house domicile ruler and almuten), the Moon.

USB stick: If the item is lost, then the second house, Venus (2nd house domicile ruler), Saturn (2nd house almuten), the Moon (conjunct the 2nd house cusp and also natural significator of lost items) . If it is mislaid, which is probably the case here, then the fourth house and Jupiter (4th house domicile ruler and almuten). However, the Moon in the 2nd house indicates perhaps that this is a 2nd house matter.

Testimonies for: The Moon applies to a trine with Mercury in domicile and he receives her. The Moon also applies to a trine with Venus, her dispositor by domicile (always a good sign in these charts). The Moon will finally apply to the other Fortune, Jupiter, ruler of the fourth house. The two Fortunes are conjunct and they are received there by domicile ruler, Mercury. Mercury has left combustion and he is very fast and direct.

Testimonies against: Mercury is under the beams (but he is in domicile). Saturn is retrograde.

Judgement: It is rare to find a fortunate chart such as this. The USB stick will most certainly be found.

Outcome: It was found a few weeks later out of the blue.

Astrological conclusions: This is a perfect example of how it doesn't often matter what the question is. It would be very difficult to give a negative answer to any question with a chart like this one.

"Will there be an agreement?"

The new Greek government of Syriza could not reach an agreement with the other member states of the European Union over the financial measures to be taken and time was running out. On the day before the question, the general consensus was that an agreement would be reached that Saturday, four days later. The day of the question, a new disagreement occurred and I cast the chart.

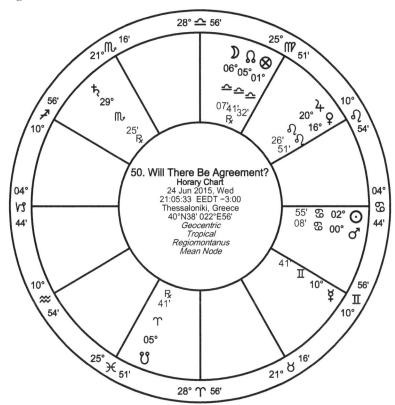

Greece: First house, Saturn (1st house domicile ruler and almuten), the Moon.

European partners: Seventh house, the Moon (7th house domicile ruler and co–almuten), Mars (7th house co–almuten and conjunct the 7th house cusp), the Sun.

Testimonies for: The Moon applies to a trine with Mercury, natural ruler of documents and communication, who is in his domicile and he receives her. The Moon is conjunct the Lot of Fortune and the North

Node. Saturn is in his own terms and has a mutual reception with Venus (face/terms). The Moon, after the trine with Mercury, will form a sextile with Venus, a Fortune, who receives her and then another sextile with Jupiter, the other Fortune. Mars is in his own triplicity and terms.

Testimonies against: Mars is in fall, combust and afflicts the 7th house. The Moon is afflicted by the Sun and Mars (she receives them, though). Saturn is retrograde. Mercury (the Moon's next aspect) is in the 6th house and Venus and Jupiter (the planets the Moon applies to after the trine with Mercury) are in the 8th house.

Judgement: Combust Mars afflicting the 7th house cusp is certainly not a good testimony. However, he has sufficient essential dignity and receives the Sun. Saturn is not in a good condition, but at least he is in his own terms and has a (weak) mutual reception with Venus. The good thing about this chart is the Moon who has nothing but fortunate aspects to look forward to. So yes, an agreement will be reached despite the problems Mars might cause. The Moon's trine to Mercury perfects in five degrees approximately and the sextile with Venus in 11 degrees.

Outcome: What happened afterwards really confirms what I always say "Stick to a yes or no answer" and leave out the details, because in many cases you will get it wrong. The Greek government left the talks with the European partners and three days later the Prime Minister called a referendum which took place 11 days after the question. Five days after the question a new proposition was made by the Europeans, but to no avail. In the referendum, the Greek people opted for no agreement with the European Union, so I thought my interpretation was wrong. However, the Prime Minister, who had apparently changed his mind in-between, took the No for a Yes (a very bizarre moment in history) and he went for an agreement. So, the day of the referendum (11 days after the question) was actually the day of the agreement. The actual agreement with all the details was announced on the 13th of July, exactly when Mars left combustion.

Astrological conclusions: This is a chart of mixed testimonies, but demonstrates the importance of the Moon in every chart. The fact that the Moon is increasing in light, with only fortunate aspects to make ahead, and in an angular sign, is a clear indication of YES.

"Will the dress fit me?"

The querent had bought a dress online, suitable for an important occasion she was planning to go to and she was anxious to know whether everything would be OK.

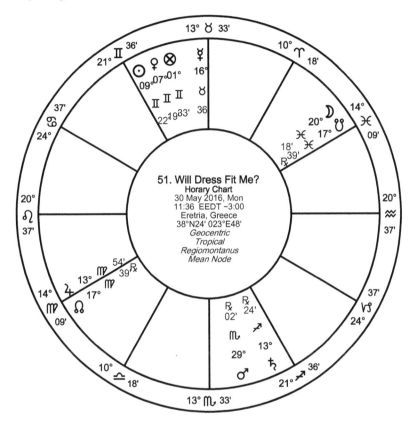

Querent: First house, the Sun (1st house domicile ruler and almuten), the Moon.

Dress: I'm not sure that we need a separate house significator for the dress, especially in this case since the querent is interested in how the dress will fit her body and she does not view it as a possession. If we regard it as a possession, then the 2nd house would be more appropriate. Since the querent had not yet paid for the dress, the dress still belonged to the seller and we should perhaps treat it as an 8th house item. The fact that the Moon is in the 8th house strengthens this view. Since Jupiter, the 8th house domicile ruler and co–almuten and also the 5th house domicile ruler and almuten, is conjunct the 2nd house cusp, we can safely use him. Clothes were usually assigned to the 5th house traditionally (they decorate the body) and Venus was the natural significator (particularly dresses, I presume). Other possible significators: Saturn (conjunct the 5th house cusp) and Mercury (2nd house domicile ruler and almuten). Anyway, it doesn't really matter, we should not make such a fuss over correct significators. It is the whole chart that will lead us to the correct answer.

Testimonies for: The Moon applies to a trine with Mars in domicile with reception. Mercury is angular in the 10th house and in a mutual reception with Venus (no aspect) and makes a trine (separating) with Jupiter with reception. The North Node is in the 2nd house. The Sun has more affinity with the fortunate 11th house, which he naturally rules following the Chaldean order of planets.

Testimonies against: The Moon is in the malefic 8th house and she's conjunct the South Node. Mars (to whom she applies) is retrograde. Jupiter, ruler of both the 5th and the 8th houses, is in detriment and afflicted by the partill square with Saturn and the square with the Sun. Saturn afflicts the 5th house by his presence. Venus is combust and applies to oppose Saturn. The Sun, principal ruler of the querent, also applies to oppose Saturn (with mutual reception though by triplicity). Mercury applies to an opposition with retrograde Mars.

Judgement: Venus is combust and applies to oppose Saturn, so the reception without aspect with Mercury will not help much. The Sun will also oppose Saturn, showing the dissatisfaction of the querent. The Moon's next aspect is a trine with Mars in domicile, but Mars' retrogradation and the Moon's conjunction with the South Node reduce the good fortune. There is no clear positive testimony in this chart, so the querent will be dissatisfied. It will probably not be a total disaster, because of the mutual reception between the Sun and Saturn and the trine between the Moon and Mars.

Outcome: The dress was a bit tight in the chest area and very hot, so she didn't wear it on the important occasion as she originally planned. She also wasn't given a receipt, which annoyed her a lot.

Astrological conclusions: No matter what the significator of the dress is, the fact that the Sun (querent) applies to oppose Saturn, an Infortune, shows her dissatisfaction.

"Will there be an agreement?"

The Greek government and our European partners were unable to reach an agreement over economic measures to be taken, and the greater the delay, the worse for the economy. (This is what happened in the summer of 2015 – see chart fifty). However, everybody hoped that there would be an agreement before Easter Day, which fell on May 1st.

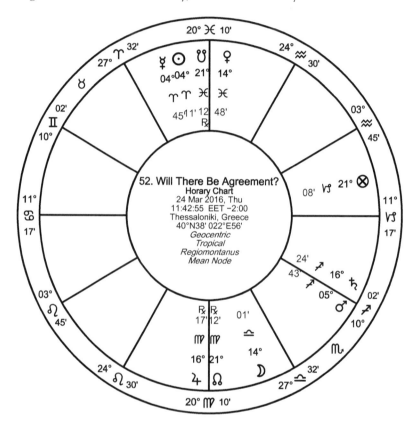

Greece: First house, the Moon (1st house domicile ruler and co–almuten), Venus (1st house co–almuten).

European partners: Seventh house, Saturn (7th house domicile ruler and co–almuten), Mars (7th house co–almuten).

Testimonies for: Venus is angular and also essentially dignified. The Moon applies to a sextile with Saturn with mutual reception. The Lot of

Fortune is in the 7th house. The Sun in exaltation applies to a trine with Mars with a strong mutual reception. Both the Fortunes are angular and they have a mutual reception. Mars is in the house of his joy.

Testimonies against: The Moon is besieged between the two Infortunes (with a fortunate sextile though) and is afflicted by her recent opposition with the Sun. Venus is conjunct the South Node. Mars and Saturn are cadent. Mars is very slow. The two Infortunes (and significators) are conjunct (the conjunction will never become exact though as Mars will turn retrograde). Venus applies to a square with Saturn (with reception, though).

Judgement: The sextile between the Moon and Saturn (the principal significators) with reception looks very promising and so does the Lot of Fortune in the 7th house. The applying trine with the Sun will help Mars a lot and Venus is very strong. Since the Moon is the applying and lighter planet, it is the Greek government who seems desperate to close the deal. However, the Venus/Saturn square raises some doubts (although Saturn is in Venus' terms and Venus herself is incredibly strong) and it may cause some problems. Perhaps this is an indication that there will be a delay. The Moon needs a little less than 2.5 degrees to perfect the aspect with Saturn, but she is very slow and it might take a little longer. Mars is also moving very slowly and this may be another indication of delay. So, weeks or months? The Moon is in a cardinal sign, but she's in a different sign from the angle and Saturn is cadent in a mutable sign. Months seem more likely, although, according to the Minister of Finance, this would be a "disaster".

Outcome: A little more than a week later (Venus square Saturn?) the Greek government released an intercepted telephone conversation between the IMF representatives, which, according to the government, showed that the IMF was trying to sabotage the deal and lead Greece to bankruptcy. The IMF denied the accusations and responded angrily. Finally, the Greek government decided to agree on everything and voted the necessary measures. On May 24th, exactly two months later, an agreement was reached, provided Greece would take some supplementary measures. These were taken on June 7th and the Euroworking group confirmed this on June 9th, two and a half months later. The final OK, in order for Greece to receive the money, was given on June 16th.

Astrological conclusions: I trust it has become evident by now, that this applying sextile with a strong reception between the Moon in Libra and Saturn in Sagittarius has never failed to produce a positive outcome. Naturally, there shouldn't be extreme negativity in the rest of the chart.

"Will she contact me?"

I hadn't heard from a client (chart fifteen in the relationships section) and I wanted to know what had happened. I sent the client two emails, but there was no answer.

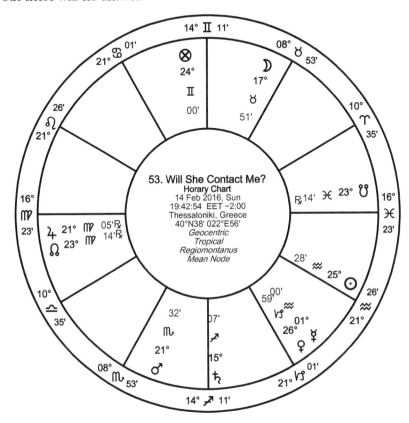

Me: First house, Mercury (1st house domicile ruler and almuten), the Moon, Jupiter, the North Node.

Client: Seventh house, Jupiter (7th house domicile ruler and almuten).

Testimonies for: The Moon is strong in the sign of her exaltation and triplicity, in her own face and she is fast. She is also in hayz. Jupiter is conjunct the North Node in the 1st house. Mercury is in his terms and triplicity, far from the Sun and has an above average speed. Jupiter has a mutual reception with dignified Mars and they form a partill sextile. The

Moon is in the turned 3rd house of communications and applying to a trine with Jupiter in the 1st house with mutual reception.

Testimonies against: The Moon is afflicted by the opposition with Mars (although Mars is probably a benefic here, since he is in his domicile and triplicity in a nocturnal chart) and the square with the Sun. Jupiter is afflicted by his square with Saturn (there is reception, though) and he is retrograde. The South Node is in the 7th house of clients. Mercury and Jupiter don't aspect each other.

Judgement: The Moon may be opposite Mars and square the Sun, but the very fortunate trine with Jupiter, the client, comes first and she has lots of dignity. My only problem was Jupiter being retrograde and his square with Saturn. However, the Moon also comes first in this case, so, although I could not see how it could happen, I was confident that I would make contact with her in the end. The Moon needs almost 3.5 degrees to trine Jupiter, although it should be sooner, as Jupiter is retrograde and the Moon is fast. The Moon is in a fixed sign and a cadent house (which probably will also delay the event), so it must be months and not weeks.

Outcome: I unexpectedly found her telephone number through another client and called her. This happened four months later. The timing is close, but slightly off, unless we take the Moon/Mars opposition to signify the contact (the radical and the turned 3rd house rulers) and Jupiter as the other client who intervened. The negativity of the opposition (although they are both extremely dignified) can be explained by the fact that I didn't learn much, as she was unwilling to go into details. She only told me that I was right and I didn't want to pressure her as the subject was particularly sensitive.

Astrological conclusions: A trine with reception is the best testimony out there.

"Will we have a baby?"

The querent had recently got married, but she was over forty and she desperately wanted to have a baby before time ran out.

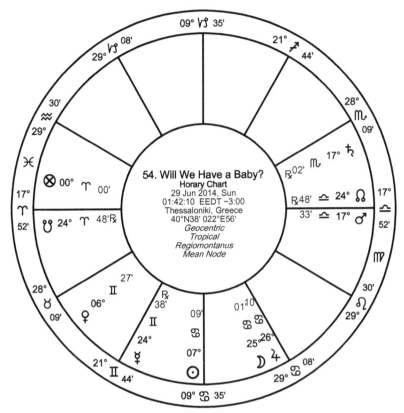

Querent: First house, Mars (1st house domicile ruler and co–almuten), the Sun (1st house co–almuten), the Moon, the South Node.

Baby: Fifth house, the Moon (5th house domicile ruler and almuten), the Sun (ruler of the majority of the degrees of the 5th house and also because Leo is the natural 5th house with an Aries ascendant), Jupiter (natural significator of pregnancy), Venus (also connected with pregnancy being the natural ruler of the 5th house, where she also rejoices).

Testimonies for: The Sun, the Moon and Jupiter are angular in fertile Cancer and the Sun is received by both the Moon and Jupiter in the sign of their domicile and exaltation respectively. The 5th house cusp is in Cancer and the Moon and Jupiter make a conjunction with it. The Moon is in her domicile and Jupiter is exalted. The Moon is free from the beams and applies to conjunct Jupiter with mutual reception. Mars and Saturn have a mutual reception (there is no aspect though and Saturn is retrograde and doesn't aspect the ascendant). Venus, a Fortune and a planet connected with pregnancy, is applying to trine Mars and she receives him.

Testimonies against: The South Node afflicts the 1st house. Mars, domicile ruler of the ascendant is in detriment and exactly conjunct the 7th house cusp, therefore afflicting the 1st/7th house axis (the querent and her husband) and also the Moon/Jupiter conjunction (although Mars is quite far). The Sun applies to square Mars (there is reception, though).

Judgement: The applying conjunction between the Moon and Jupiter in Cancer is an extremely fortunate testimony in any chart, but especially in a pregnancy question, and can leave no doubt that there is going to be a pregnancy. However, angular Mars in detriment (despite the – not particularly helpful – mutual reception with Saturn) afflicting the 1st/7th house axis and squaring the Sun could cause problems. The South Node in the 1st house is also problematic. The conjunction between the Moon and Jupiter perfects in 1 degree and 10 minutes, but the Moon is very slow and the event may take longer. Since the conjunction is angular and Cancer is a cardinal (moveable) sign, it must happen very quickly. A week? A month at the most – unless the problems indicated by angular Mars in detriment cause a delay. Also, Venus needs to travel 17 degrees approximately to perfect the trine with Mars (Venus is fast though and the event may happen sooner).

Outcome: Well, it was not a week, nor a month, but a year! She had to undergo IVF treatments and the third time it was successful. She got pregnant in early October 2015, a year and three months after the question (the conjunction needed more than one degree to perfect and the trine between Venus and Mars also agrees) and gave birth to a baby boy in the summer of 2016.

Astrological conclusions: Nothing can beat a Moon/Jupiter conjunction in Cancer in a pregnancy question.

"Will I win in court? Will I get monetary compensation?"
The querent was fired from her job while pregnant, which is against the law. She filed a complaint against her former employer. Another question first asked to another astrologer.

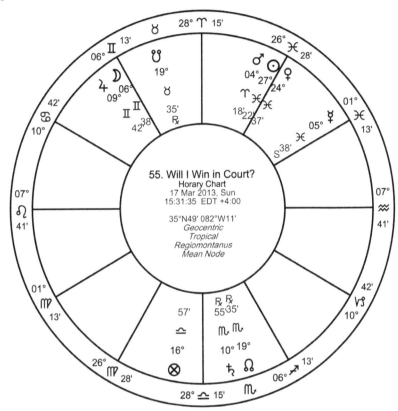

Querent: First house, the Sun (1st house domicile ruler and almuten), the Moon.

Adversary: Seventh house, Saturn (7th house domicile ruler and almuten).

Judge: Tenth house, Mars (10th house domicile ruler), the Sun (10th house almuten).

Querent's money: Second house, Mercury (2nd house domicile ruler and almuten), the Lot of Fortune, Venus (domicile ruler of the Lot of Fortune), Saturn (almuten of the Lot of Fortune), Jupiter (natural significator of wealth).

Testimonies for: The Sun is received by Venus in the sign of her exaltation and triplicity. The Sun also has a strong mutual reception with Mars (exaltation, triplicity/terms, face). The Moon is in the fortunate 11th house and applies to conjunct Jupiter, a Fortune, in his terms and face. The judge is dignified (Mars in Aries and the Sun has strong receptions) and so he will probably proceed according to the law. Saturn, the adversary, is retrograde and peregrine. Mercury, the domicile ruler and almuten of the 2nd house, is stationary and about to turn direct. Mercury also has a strong mutual reception with Jupiter.

Testimonies against: The Sun is cadent. Both rulers of the Lot of Fortune (Venus and Saturn) are in a poor condition. Venus is combust (though dignified) and Saturn is retrograde and peregrine. Jupiter, the planet the Moon applies to and domicile ruler of the 8th house (the employer's money) is in detriment. Mercury is in the sign of his detriment and fall and in the 8th house.

Judgement: The fact that the Moon is applying to a Fortune with dignity is a positive testimony. The adversary doesn't seem strong and the judge is fair. So, the odds are in her favour and she must win. There is a serious problem with the money, though. All the significators of money are debilitated. Either the court will not award her a lot of money or she won't be able to collect it.

Outcome: She won the case and she was awarded a significant sum of money. She hasn't been able, however, to collect it thus far. The company shut down and her former employer doesn't seem to have any possessions to his name.

Astrological conclusions: The Moon applying to a Fortune with dignity is always a good thing.

Part Nine
The Sequence of the Planets
in the Egyptian Bounds

When I got into traditional astrology some years ago, I came across a form of essential dignity called terms (or bounds). In short, each planet (with the exception of the Lights) is supposed to have dignity in certain degrees of every sign. What was strange about terms was that everybody said they worked, but the logic behind the table was lost in time and despite the efforts made by contemporary astrologers, no sufficient explanation could be given either about the sequence of the planets or about the number of the allotted degrees. What also creates a lot of difficulties is the fact that several tables of terms/bounds exist, especially variations of Ptolemy's table. There doesn't seem to be any disagreement among authors, however, regarding the sequence of the planets in the Egyptian bounds.

So, which table to use? That was left up to the individual, based on purely personal, therefore subjective, preferences. Those horary astrologers whose studies are based mostly on Lilly's work use Ptolemy's terms (or at least Lilly's variation of Ptolemy's terms), usually with no questions asked. The Hellenistic astrologers prefer the Egyptian bounds, because they don't like the changes (with the exception of primary directions) Ptolemy made in Hellenistic astrology in general. The bizarre excuse Ptolemy offered, that he found his own version of the terms in an old book of an unnamed author, didn't help much either. I also started using the Egyptian bounds for the same reasons. It is extremely difficult to prove which set of terms works better, but if I could at least understand the sequence of the planets (forget about the number of degrees allotted), I would be satisfied.

Before we go any further, what are the obvious facts? Firstly, both Lights are excluded from this form of dignity and only the five planets have bounds. Is there a reason behind this exclusion? The obvious one seems to stem from the fact that the number of degrees each planet gets has to coincide with the number of years they are allotted in traditional

The Sequence of the Planets in the Egyptian Bounds

♈	0	♃	6	♀	12	☿	20	♂	25	♄	30
♉	0	♀	8	☿	14	♃	22	♄	27	♂	30
♊	0	☿	6	♃	12	♀	17	♂	24	♄	30
♋	0	♂	7	♀	13	☿	18	♃	26	♄	30
♌	0	♃	6	♀	11	♄	18	☿	24	♂	30
♍	0	☿	7	♀	17	♃	21	♂	28	♄	30
♎	0	♄	6	☿	14	♃	21	♀	28	♂	30
♏	0	♂	7	♀	11	☿	19	♃	24	♄	30
♐	0	♃	12	♀	17	☿	21	♄	26	♂	30
♑	0	☿	7	♃	14	♀	22	♄	26	♂	30
♒	0	☿	7	♀	13	♃	20	♂	25	♄	30
♓	0	♀	12	♃	16	☿	19	♂	28	♄	30

astrology. Which set of years though? The least, the mean or the greater one? Keeping in mind that the final number has to be 360 (the degrees of the whole zodiac), if you add up all the years in each set, only the mean set comes close to 360 (356 to be precise), but close is not exact. If you take out the degrees of the Lights however, the total of the number of greater years of the five planets is 360 (57+66+79+82+76 = 360).

Another possible reason for the exclusion of the Lights could be that the Lights in traditional astrology do not seem to "cause" things. They do not signify "manners" or "character", nor do they show the native's "profession". Instead, they seem to be beyond these things. The Sun seems to be the source of everything and the Moon brings the planets together. The Lights are not "active" parts of the horoscope, which means that the term ruler needs to be active, and therefore a planet and not a luminary. This seems to place emphasis on the terms and make them a special form of dignity.

Secondly, the Infortunes are primarily placed at the end of the signs (in both tables that is). Thirdly, just like in Ptolemy's terms, Mars and Saturn seem to play the part of domicile ruler in Cancer and Leo accordingly, in view of the absence of the Sun and Moon. I would go even further and say that, as a result of the change of rulerships, Saturn's sign of detriment (only for the bounds, naturally) is Aquarius and Mars' is Capricorn. Finally, face rulership seems to play an important part in times of indecision.

Here is – in my opinion – the logic behind the sequence of the planets in the Egyptian bounds.

Sequence of the planets

1) **The first column** is a place for what I call the triplicity almuten, that is, the planet that has the most dignity in all three signs of a single triplicity. In the fire triplicity, with the absence of the Sun, the most dignified planet there is Jupiter (domicile rulership in Sagittarius and triplicity rulership by night). In the water triplicity, Mars is the most dignified planet because he has two domicile rulerships (Cancer, Scorpio) and triplicity rulership by night. Since Saturn doesn't rule Aquarius, Mercury is the most dignified planet in the air triplicity (domicile rulership in Gemini and triplicity rulership by night). Saturn has exaltation and triplicity rulership, but domicile rulership tops exaltation. Finally, in the earth triplicity Mercury is again the overall triplicity ruler (rulership and exaltation in Virgo). Venus has domicile and triplicity rulership in the earth signs, but exaltation is preferred over triplicity and Mercury wins. **However, if there is a planet that has double major dignity in a particular sign, then that planet is preferred for that sign only.** More specifically:

Jupiter is given first place in all the fire signs because he is the triplicity almuten and there is no other planet with more dignity than him in any of the three signs.

Mercury is the triplicity almuten in the earth signs, so he is given the first place in the earth signs with the exception of Taurus, where Venus is preferred because she has double dignity in Taurus (domicile rulership and triplicity rulership).

Mercury is given first place in the air signs with the exception of Libra, where Saturn is preferred because he has double dignity there (exaltation and triplicity rulership).

Mars is the triplicity almuten in water, so he is given first place there with the exception of Pisces, where Venus has double dignity (exaltation and triplicity rulership).

2) **The second column** is the column of the Fortunes. Only Venus or Jupiter can be placed here, **unless the triplicity almuten wasn't used in the first column** and has to be placed here. However, if the triplicity almuten that wasn't used in the first column is an Infortune, he can't be used, as this place is only for the two Fortunes. In the case where neither Fortune was used in the first column, we choose the Fortune that is a face ruler in that particular sign.

So, in all the fire signs the only choice is Venus, because she is the only Fortune left, as Jupiter was used in the first column in all three signs.

In the earth signs: Mercury, the triplicity almuten, wasn't used in the first column in Taurus, because of Venus' double dignity, so he will take second place. In Virgo and Capricorn we have to make a choice between Venus and Jupiter. Venus is preferred in Virgo and Jupiter in Capricorn (face rulers).

In the air signs: In Libra, Mercury, the triplicity almuten, wasn't used because of Saturn's double dignity, so he takes second place. In Gemini and Aquarius we have to make a choice between Venus and Jupiter. In Gemini, Jupiter is preferred and in Aquarius, Venus (face rulers).

In the water signs: In Pisces, Venus took first place, so only one Fortune is left – Jupiter – who takes second place. Mars, the overall triplicity ruler can't be used here, as he is an Infortune. In Cancer and Scorpio we have to make a choice between Venus and Jupiter. In both cases, Venus is the face ruler, so she takes second place.

3) **The third column** is the column of the non–Infortune planet that is still left. In the case where two non–Infortune planets are still left, the face ruler is again preferred.

In the fire signs, Mercury is the only non–Infortune planet left, so he gets third place in Sagittarius and Aries. In Leo, however, Saturn takes third place, because as Leo's ruler, he functions as a non–Infortune in this sign and therefore we have two non–Infortunes left, Saturn and Mercury. Saturn, as a face ruler, gets third place.

In the earth signs, the non–Infortune planet still left is used.

In the air signs the same, but in Libra we have two non–Infortunes still left, Venus and Jupiter. Jupiter will be used as he is the face ruler.

Water signs: In Pisces, the non–Infortune still left – Mercury – is used. In Cancer and Scorpio, we have two non–Infortunes still left. In Cancer, Mercury prevails as the face ruler. In Scorpio, neither Mercury nor Jupiter is a face ruler. Jupiter, as a superior planet, will take fourth place (the last two columns befit more the superior planets) and Mercury will take third place.

4) **The last two columns** are places of the Infortunes. The non–Infortune still left will take fourth place.

In Cancer, Leo and Libra we have a non–Infortune still left, so they will take fourth place. Between Mars and Saturn, the general order is Mars (the less superior) in the fourth place and Saturn in the fifth, unless Saturn is a face ruler, in which case he will take fourth place (Taurus, Sagittarius). In Pisces, they are both face rulers, so the general order is kept and that is also the case in Aquarius, where neither of them is a face ruler. Capricorn is a special case here. Since Mars is a face ruler in Capricorn, he should have taken fourth place, but that isn't the case. If this isn't a mistake (which I suspect it is), it may be that detriment was taken into account here. Mars, by ruling Cancer, is in detriment in Capricorn and so he takes last place as the greater Infortune in this particular sign. The fact that Saturn takes last place in Aquarius, where one perhaps would expect him to take fourth place, in spite of him not having face rulership there, also corroborates this.

The number of degrees

I haven't been able to solve this puzzle and I'm not even sure there is some great puzzle to be solved. There is a total number of degrees (360) that has to be divided in 12 signs and 5 planets but not equally, because each planet has a different number of degrees to cover. So adjustments were made. I have, however, a few ideas, as to what sort of rules were possibly followed for this procedure.

1) The two benefics in the first column double their average degrees (12), in signs where they have double dignity. This can

happen only once however, because it would be problematic if a planet had 24 degrees in only two signs, as there would be very few left for the other ten signs. For Jupiter, this is not a problem, as he has double dignity only in one sign in the first column, Sagittarius (domicile and triplicity). Venus, however, has double dignity in two signs, Taurus and Pisces. I believe that Pisces was chosen in the end, because exaltation is more specific than domicile rulership, since it concerns only one particular sign. These extra degrees of Jupiter and Venus are deducted from the other two signs of the same triplicity, Jupiter's degrees from Leo and Aries (8–2 = 6) and Venus' degrees from Scorpio and Cancer (6–2 = 4).

2)   As a general rule, planets get more degrees in signs they rule (with the exception of the Infortunes because of the change of rulerships), in signs they are exalted, or in signs they are triplicity rulers. Adjustments are made based on what planet it is and which column they are in. Mercury, for example, is often found in the first column (where he rules two signs), so he can't get eight degrees for each sign.

3)   Planets lose two degrees on average in their signs of detriment (Mars' detriment is in Capricorn and Saturn's detriment is in Aquarius). Venus and Jupiter have a lot of degrees to cover, so this deduction is made in only one of their signs of detriment. Planets do not seem to lose points when located in the signs of their fall.

4)   If a planet is the overall triplicity ruler, but could not be placed in the first three columns of one of their signs, they get extra degrees. For example, Mars was not put in the first column in Pisces because of Venus and could not be put in the second and third column either, because he is an Infortune. However, he is not only a triplicity ruler in water, but he is also the overall triplicity ruler. Hence the nine degrees he is allotted.

5)   For some reason, Mars gets extra degrees in Mercury–ruled signs and Mercury gets extra degrees in Mars–ruled signs, while Jupiter gets extra degrees in Venus' signs. However, Venus can't do the same in Jupiter–ruled signs, because she already has 12 degrees in Pisces and Jupiter has 12 degrees in Sagittarius, so there needs to be a deduction of degrees from the other planets in Sagittarius, as is the case

in Pisces as well. Perhaps, this is because of the friendly (sextile) relationship that exists between the signs they normally rule (Gemini and Virgo sextile Aries and Scorpio, while Taurus and Libra sextile Pisces and Sagittarius), but Mars here is supposed to rule Cancer. Anyway, I don't really know.

I would be very pleased to find out what other people's thoughts are on this subject.

Bibliography

Al Biruni. *The Book of Instruction in the Elements of the Art of Astrology*, Astrology Classics, 2006.

Culpeper, Nicholas. *Astrological Judgement of Diseases from the Decumbiture of the Sick*, Astrology Classics, 2003.

Dunn, Barbara. *Horary Astrology Re-Examined*, Wessex Astrologer, 2009.

Dykes, Ben. *Bonatti on Horary*, The Cazimi Press, 2010.
_____ *The Forty Chapters of Al-Kindi*, The Cazimi Press, 2011.
_____ *The Book of the Nine Judges*, The Cazimi Press, 2011.
_____ *Works of Sahl and Masha'allah*, The Cazimi Press, 2008.

Ezra, Rabbi Avraham Ibn. *The Book of Nativities and Revolutions*, Arhat Publications, 2008.

Hand, Robert. *Whole Sign Houses, The Oldest House System*, Arhat Publications, 2000.
_____ *Night & Day, Planetary Sect in Astrology*, Arhat Publications, 1995.

Houlding, Deborah. *The Houses, Temples of the Sky*, The Wessex Astrologer, 2006.

Lehman, J. Lee. *The Book of Rulerships*, Whitford Press, 1992.

Lilly, Wiliam. *Christian Astrology, Books 1 & 2*, Astrology Classics, 2004.

Masha'allah. *On Reception*, Arhat Publications, 1998.
Ptolemy, Claudius. *Tetrabiblos (Books A, B, C, D)*, Cactus Editions, 2001.

Saunders, Richard. *The Astrological Judgement and Practice of Physick*, Astrology Classics, 2003.

Other Titles from The Wessex Astrologer
www.wessexastrologer.com

Martin Davis
Astrolocality Astrology: A Guide to What it is and How to Use it
From Here to There: An Astrologer's Guide to Astromapping

Wanda Sellar
The Consultation Chart
An Introduction to Medical Astrology
An Introduction to Decumbiture

Geoffrey Cornelius
The Moment of Astrology

Darrelyn Gunzburg
Life After Grief: An Astrological Guide to Dealing with Grief
AstroGraphology: The Hidden Link between your Horoscope and your Handwriting

Paul F. Newman
Declination: The Steps of the Sun
Luna: The Book of the Moon

Deborah Houlding
The Houses: Temples of the Sky

Dorian Geiseler Greenbaum
Temperament: Astrology's Forgotten Key

Howard Sasportas
The Gods of Change

Patricia L. Walsh
Understanding Karmic Complexes

M. Kelly Hunter
Living Lilith: the Four Dimensions of the Cosmic Feminine

Barbara Dunn
Horary Astrology Re-Examined

Deva Green
Evolutionary Astrology

Jeff Green
Pluto Volume 1: The Evolutionary Journey of the Soul
Pluto Volume 2: The Evolutionary Journey of the Soul Through Relationships
Essays on Evolutionary Astrology (ed. by Deva Green)

Dolores Ashcroft-Nowicki and Stephanie V. Norris
The Door Unlocked: An Astrological Insight into Initiation

Greg Bogart
Astrology and Meditation: The Fearless Contemplation of Change

Henry Seltzer
The Tenth Planet: Revelations from the Astrological Eris

Ray Grasse
Under a Sacred Sky: Essays on the Practice and Philosophy of Astrology

Martin Gansten
Primary Directions

Joseph Crane
Astrological Roots: The Hellenistic Legacy
Between Fortune and Providence

Bruce Scofield
Day-Signs: Native American Astrology from Ancient Mexico

Komilla Sutton
The Essentials of Vedic Astrology
The Lunar Nodes: Crisis and Redemption
Personal Panchanga: The Five Sources of Light
The Nakshatras: the Stars Beyond the Zodiac

Anthony Louis
The Art of Forecasting using Solar Returns

Reina James
All the Sun Goes Round: Tales from the Zodiac

Oscar Hofman
Classical Medical Astrology

Bernadette Brady
Astrology, A Place in Chaos
Star and Planet Combinations

Richard Idemon
The Magic Thread
Through the Looking Glass

Nick Campion
The Book of World Horoscopes

Judy Hall
Patterns of the Past
Karmic Connections
Good Vibrations
The Soulmate Myth: A Dream Come True or Your Worst Nightmare?
The Book of Why: Understanding your Soul's Journey
Book of Psychic Development

Neil D. Paris
Surfing your Solar Cycles

Michele Finey
The Sacred Dance of Venus and Mars

David Hamblin
The Spirit of Numbers

Dennis Elwell
Cosmic Loom

Gillian Helfgott
The Insightful Turtle

Bob Makransky
Planetary Strength
Planetary Hours
Planetary Combination

CPSIA information can be obtained
at www.ICGtesting.com
Printed in the USA
BVHW041205011219
565295BV00003B/17/P